En...

I have had the privilege to kno...
attending Pioneer Bible Chur...
love, and consistent service to Christ continues to be genuine and
passionate. Kendra truly wants each individual to be all that she/
he can be for Christ. This includes gifts, abilities, passions, and
aspirations.

In this book, she desires to encourage, motivate, and strengthen
the reader to have action steps for a fruitful life that will be
deeply satisfying and give glory to God. You will find her writing
practical, relatable, and real. Kendra desires to come alongside
you to give you the inspiration, motivation, and practical steps
to more successfully use your God-given gifts to love Christ,
bringing your unique abilities to serve and help others.

Kendra loves the Word of God, and brings helpful and intentional
scriptures to keep you grounded and leaning upon God for His
strength as you live and live out your dreams. Enjoy her heartfelt
testimony, true stories, and God-honoring process, as you journey
to fulfill your God-given call to His Glory.

~Pastor, Jim Eggert, Pioneer Bible Church,
Somerset, California

With her insightful and ministry-driven heart, author Kendra
Carroll will challenge and inspire her readers to discover ways to
serve God by serving others. A perennial encourager, Kendra's
book will inspire Christians who are searching to walk more
closely with God in their daily lives.

~Lisa M. Whitaker, Lavish Leadership Educator,
Columnist and Speaker

Step Into Your Calling has helped me not only in my business,
but also in my personal life! Kendra has an amazing ability to
not only help steward who God created you to be, but also helps

1

inspire new ideas for those already walking in their calling. The book, journaling prompts along with her coaching help you define your passions and who God made you to be!! This book is one you will want to read and journal over and over as you walk through different seasons in your life and calling!

~Beth Leanna Cline, CEO Leanna Cosmetics, Speaker of Faith and Business, Producer and Director of Glory Network

While reading this book, I felt like Kendra was speaking directly to me. She touches everything a person faces when starting and navigating a ministry and/or business. Her encouragement is contagious and will definitely spread beyond the pages of this book!

~Britt Topp, The Blended Homemaker

When Kendra first told me she was writing a book encouraging God's calling, especially in the business setting, I didn't know if her words would apply to me. I am not a business woman, I am "just" a mom. God has called me to my family and the work within our home. Kendra has spent countless hours uplifting me, reminding me that no calling is too small if it's God's calling. She wraps each individual in the knowledge that God smiles on each and everyone of our efforts.

~Jessica B., wife, mother, Jesus Sister

Kendra saw in me what I couldn't fully see in myself. She gave direction to a calling of which I was unsure where to go with. Her God Gift is to be a beacon for others to see their own God Gift and through the words in this book she broadens the field and shines even brighter for all who read them!

~Charlie Bogaczyk, future author of Inspired By Angels & "Visions From Underneath"

I read *Step Into Your Calling* and it changed my life. Kendra Dee

Carroll's words helped me put things into perspective to prioritize the purpose that God has for me.

I know this book will be helpful to anyone who reads it. Whoever is wondering what their purpose is, what's their strengths and weaknesses, what you should be doing, it's all covered in this book. This book is an overall encouragement to who you are in Christ.

-Denise Williams (The Romanticist Writer,
Writing with God Coach)

Step Into Your Calling—Copyright © 2024 by Kendra Carroll
Published by UNITED HOUSE Publishing

All rights reserved. No portion of this book may be reproduced or shared in any form–electronic, printed, photocopied, recording, or by any information storage and retrieval system, without prior written permission from the publisher. The use of short quotations is permitted.

ISBN: 978-1-952840-43-2

UNITED HOUSE Publishing
Waterford, Michigan
info@unitedhousepublishing.com
www.unitedhousepublishing.com

Photographer Credits: Sheila King of Sheila King Photography https://www.sheilakingphotography.com/

Scripture quotations marked (NIV) are taken from the Holy Bible, New International Version®, NIV®. Copyright © 1973, 1978, 1984, 2011 by Biblica, Inc.™ Used by permission of Zondervan. All rights reserved worldwide. www.zondervan.comThe "NIV" and "New International Version" are trademarks registered in the United States Patent and Trademark Office by Biblica, Inc.™

Scripture quotations marked (NLT) are taken from the Holy Bible, New Living Translation, copyright ©1996, 2004, 2015 by Tyndale House Foundation. Used by permission of Tyndale House Publishers, Carol Stream, Illinois 60188. All rights reserved.

"Scripture quotations are from the ESV® Bible (The Holy Bible, English Standard Version®), copyright © 2001 by Crossway, a publishing ministry of Good News Publishers. Used by permission. All rights reserved. The ESV text may not be quoted in any publication made available to the public by a Creative Commons license. The ESV may not be translated in whole or in part into any other language."

Scripture quotations marked (NKJV) are taken from the New King James Version. Copyright © 1982 by Thomas Nelson, Inc. Used by permission. All rights reserved. Bible text from the New King James Version® is not to be reproduced in copies or otherwise by any means except as permitted in writing by Thomas Nelson, Inc., Attn: Bible Rights and Permissions, P.O. Box 141000, Nashville, TN 37214-1000.

Published in Waterford, MI
Printed in the United States
2024—First Edition
SPECIAL SALES
Most UNITED HOUSE books are available at special quantity discounts when purchased in bulk by corporations,
organizations, and special-interest groups. For information, please e-mail orders@unitedhousepublishing.com

Dedication

I dedicate this book to my husband, who unknowingly played into the call of God, to my family, who had to endure this book, and to all the readers who desire to be in God's full "yes", no matter what it looks like! This is for all of you.

Step INTO YOUR Calling

overcome doubt and discover what God has for you

Kendra Dee Carroll

Contents

Foreword

God Showed You the Vision

Have you ever had a thought or idea that you believed was amazing and at the same time unfathomable? Perhaps it was an image of something that could change the lives of many, or perhaps even change the world. Maybe what you saw was so big that you did not believe you could accomplish it. Nevertheless, God showed you what the finished product would look like. Even though it may be a surprise or mystery to you, there is a reason that God chose and entrusted you with this foreshadowing of the future. It is because Father God the Creator knows that He designed you to take the vision He showed you off the canvas of your mind and paint it on the tapestry of reality. God showed it to you and only you know what it looks like when its completed. Don't be discouraged or dismayed by the obstacles you may face. Just know and believe that before God showed you the vision, He equipped you, in the womb, to bring it to His expected end. This book by Kendra Dee Carroll intends to impart inspiration into the reader that will cause you to trust and believe that the God who gave you the vision is greater than the challenges that the journey includes. Remember, you can do all things Through Christ who strengthens you. Eyes may not have seen it yet, but that's only because Gods bringing it to pass through you.

Apostle Stephen Thompson
Founder and Senior Pastor of House of Triumph Outreach and Worship Center

Getting Started

God has a purpose with our lives, whether it's a calling to write a book, start a business, go on a mission, start a ministry, or even start a family. This book is to help you overcome the fears or doubts in the way of getting to the next steps of your calling. God calls each of us to unique and special tasks. Yes, God has created you with talents to meet the needs of His people. He has a specific assigned place where he wants to reach the people He has intended for you to serve. Whatever you are called to do will be your own journey, much like the steps of faith into entrepreneurship, because it's you and God; there is no other boss above you in life beyond what God calls you to do. As you seek only God's voice to step into your calling, it becomes a solo mission. This will begin the process of discovering who God made you to be, who you are to serve, and what He has for you to accomplish.

Although this book has some entrepreneurial stories, the stories better portray how you can represent Jesus in all you do. Anything and everything can be used for the Kingdom of God. This is a journey of self, discovering skills and talents to use for serving others. My personal journey of entrepreneurship has been more of a place for self-development where I have found how to use all of my talents, discovered new skills to serve others, and put them together to be better used by God. This journey of seeking your calling stirs from an internal place of God prompting that something is missing or the need to add more to your life. I know in my career as a horse trainer, which evolved into working with kids in leadership development, to writing this book and serving women entrepreneurs and creators of ministry, it all was a process of discovering I was made for more. Maybe you're driven by passion or seeking more purpose, but you feel an overall sense of wanting to step out in faith to obey where God is calling you. As I've continued to grow my talents and gifts through my passion to help others grow in confidence, Godly leadership, and building businesses, my territory of who I serve has also expanded. The opportunity for growth comes from letting go of what it looks like right now and leaning into the nudging that is saying, "Just try it." An entrepreneur's mentality comes with a whole lot of, "Just try it!" and your walk of faith to your calling needs the same motto. But even with the motivation and gumption we carry in our hearts, worry, fear, and doubt find ways to creep in and try to hold us back. Overcoming doubt is what moves you forward, and with God at your side as your guide, this act of trusting God to walk in your calling exercises your faith muscle. This is the faith to believe in yourself, that God has equipped you and made you for the calling you are pursuing. This is the faith that builds your trust in the Lord as you see His faithfulness show up in your efforts toward your calling, business, ministry, and life.

The "just try it" mentality leads you to where you need to go next. Even if it isn't quite right, God takes your efforts and steers them in the right direction. Sometimes, God brings just the right people to help us get to our next steps in the journey and process of who we are becoming. Other times, it is just the right circumstances that provide the opportunities. These are the types of stories you will hear about in this book. Stories about how it all worked out by letting God lead every situation and circumstance.

"Look at the birds of the air; they do not sow or reap or store away in barns, and yet your heavenly Father feeds them. Are you not much more valuable than they?"
Matthew 6:26, NIV

Keep Working

When my husband and I encourage others in entrepreneurship, we have deep discussions over this verse. His concern is someone would read this verse and do nothing, thinking God will show up and do all the work for them. I think of it like this: God put the worm in the ground, and it is up to the birds (us) to go find it. But, we thank God He put the worm there because, without Him, the worm wouldn't exist at all! The same goes for us. God places everything we need around us, but it is up to us to do the work to find those blessings and remain faithful to the work He called us to. The good thing is, we aren't doing this alone. We are constantly asking God questions and letting Him show up in our lives, ministries, and businesses. We recognize God gives us blessings and builds our confidence as He shapes us in our businesses. He is the Guide, the Boss, and the Provider. In Hebrew, "Jehovah Jireh" means "Our Lord the Provider," remember to trust Him. We need not fear, nor worry. This book is meant to help grow our trust in God's faithfulness to show up in all the ways He is calling us.

"You see, his faith and his actions worked together. His actions made his faith complete."
James 2:22, NLT

Sometimes pursuing your calling feels like you are putting in too much effort or you are digging in all the wrong places. At times, you may be looking and looking, ready to give up. Then, you turn around, and there is a worm crawling right next to you! I believe that is how God shows up. He brings the people, opportunities, and resources to add to your talents, to serve others in His name. You do the work with an expectant heart and know He will provide all you need along the way. This is where you are putting God in your business, praying over every step, and thanking Him for every gift and blessing provided.

We also have to keep doing God's business. We are in the business of growing God's mission and kingdom and spreading His Word. Not only are we asking God to help us in our business, but God's business—His message—needs to shine through in all we do to represent God in our business. God is in everything; He is here for us. We need to not separate Him into compartments any longer. For ALL we do is for the glory of the Lord. Your mission and calling are not just prayer and holding your Bible. Others will find God through the way you serve them. 90 percent of our serving is done outside the church walls in businesses, with families, friends, or even volunteer work for your community. We are called to be servants to all. Serving happens all day long. So, make sure God is the business, God is in the business, and see how God uses all He has called you to.

As you build your faith to gain the assurance God is in this with you, and you realize it is not all on you, you can begin to rely more on His provisions. It's learning to lean on God as your provider, walking in His faithfulness as you faithfully and fervently pray for His provision throughout your entire journey.

No matter if you are just thinking of beginning on this road, you're a few years in, or you've been traveling for more than a decade, this journey is all God and you! This book is full of success stories and words of encouragement to help you overcome doubts and fears and replace them with confident steps into your calling. Finding encouragement or inspiration from others can be few and far in between. It can feel very lonely because nobody else is doing your business, life, or ministry. You followed God's lead, and you're the boss of you, and there are no other directions, input, or "that-a-girl"s coming your way. You have to show up in your calling even when you don't feel like it. As freeing and wonderful as that is, sometimes an outside word of advice or encouragement would be nice. It would be nice for someone to say you are on the right road, doing the right thing. It's easy to get too much in your head, questioning everything instead of just moving forward. That's why I wrote this book. To remind you you're not alone; others have stepped out into their calling, and it is a process to endure. The feelings that will arise are normal, and there is a way to get through them and use God's instructions and guidance as you continue to discover all He has in store for you. I pray this book meets you as an encouragement in your wavering emotions, surrendered weaknesses, and every breakthrough to overcome as you are led to all God has for you as you step into your calling.

The Way the Book Works

In this book, you will be met with my questions about how I ask God what He is doing in my life. The questions I mull over are then met with Biblical truths to support how God was and is answering my heart and building confidence in me. After the Bible study section, I ask you to put your doubts and questions before the Lord. After a chance for personal reflection and journaling, the next few pages have a "backstory" to help you gain more knowledge and insight in that area. How deep you dive is entirely up to you. Whatever way you choose, do what is best for you. I've been in the busy momma season of needing a crash-course Bible study and "how-to's" without the time to dig into a deeper "backstory," but I encourage you to journal even if it's a quick thought. God will take your acknowledgment of the areas to work in and do the growing that is needed. Like everything in life, trust the process of how God is forming and directing you on your road to your calling. As you take this journey, I pray you will find new confidence as well as stronger faith and trust. May God take your whole heart, everything He has called you to, and all your efforts, and bring you success.

Chapter One

Discovering how you will serve through your gifts, for your calling, takes a lot of grace as you continue to put yourself out there for the world to find you, meet you, and get to know your skills and talents.

Have you ever thought, "Maybe I should try something new?" Or have you started something and it feels like there is another step?

That's where I'm sitting right now, wondering if my feelings are correct. It feels like it is time to take another step forward, but I question, *"Is it right? Is it the time now? Did I create this step on my own accord, or is this God's direction? Am I walking more toward what God wants me to do? Am I ready? What if I try it and I fail? But what if God just wants me to have 'learning experiences' so I grow?"*

Okay, I know that is a lot of questions, but I can't be the only girl who sits and asks God questions from every single angle I can think of because I want to do it the right way . . . His way!

I ask the questions, then I seek the answers in the Bible and prayer . . .

God answers, "Stop fearing so much, child. Don't you knock, and I open the door for you?"
  But he said to me, "My grace is sufficient for you, for my

*power is made perfect in weakness." Therefore I will boast
all the more gladly about my weaknesses, so that
Christ's power may rest on me.*
2 Corinthians 12:9, NIV

Only by God's grace can we take the next step, both in obedience
and opportunity.

Understanding "Grace and Opportunity"

Taking a step towards anything unknown can make it difficult to
trust what God has prepared for you. Nothing captures this fear
better than the uncertainty of going into business for yourself.
Choosing to be an entrepreneur means you are stepping out into
the unknown. That can be a nerve-racking experience, to say the
least.

While my husband, Dustin, was teaching at a farrier trade school,
he had a student who was also a Christian and a longtime friend.
As soon as she was out of horseshoeing school and ready to start
her new career, she instead decided to go back to her previous job,
making wedding flower arrangements. We were confused by her
lack of confidence to move forward in becoming a farrier. We told
her how good she was at horseshoeing and reminded her at one
point she felt horseshoeing was the right path for her. "Why do
you not want to walk in the opportunity of becoming a farrier that
God has opened before you?" we asked her.

Walking into the unknown can be scary and can certainly make
you feel nervous, uncomfortable, and unqualified. You begin to
second guess everything: *Am I equipped enough? Do I have this
skill?* These thoughts might make you believe the job is too big,
and you may slink back.

When we questioned her, she answered with those exact fears and doubts: "What if I'm not good enough? What if I screw up and the horse is lame forever? I'm not as good as I should be yet."

We responded, "Do you think Dustin was *the best* when he first started? Do you think he never made any mistakes? Do you think he knew exactly what to do in every situation? Do you think, even after nineteen years, he knows everything? No way!"

We learn as we go. Having experience in the field, failing, and asking questions leads to learning. As you step forward, you continue to seek knowledge. You look to others who have gone before you. You can get help when you need it, but you have to put in the work to gain further experience and grow from it.

I summed it up like this: "You have to have enough trust that you heard God correctly, that He is leading you in all circumstances, and that He won't leave you even in this. You give your best and KNOW that God will take care of the rest."

Even after the stories of all the times my husband failed, she was still filled with so much doubt. She feared the possibility of it would be much worse for her, and she worried she wouldn't have the opportunity to get better. She still thought she needed to be the best before she was on her own. I explained that even in business, God is there. I told her, "God will take every effort you put into developing this business. Don't worry about being perfect; He will shape the imperfections and use them for who you are becoming. He will be with you as you grow into your business and the more He has in store for you, all the blessings still to come. God takes empty hands and makes something out of nothing. God will guide you in business just like He has in life! Trust His faithfulness. Let go of perfection. God didn't call you to do anything perfect; you are always a work in progress. For in your weaknesses, He is made strong. He will take your best and meet you in the REST!"

But he said to me, "My grace is sufficient for you, for my power is made perfect in weakness." Therefore I will boast all the more gladly of my weaknesses, so that the power of Christ may rest on me.
2 Corinthians 12:9, NIV

The word "grace" can be interchanged as "favor" in some Bible verses. Favor and grace represent God's kindness—His special gift and blessing to us. I have heard it said this way: "Grace (favor) is giving us the ability to do something which is humanly impossible for us to do."[1] So, if we live every day by doing everything under the banner of grace, we can watch God do the impossible through us, remembering all things are for God and by God. It's mentally reminding yourself God is God, and I am human. He can do all the things I cannot! And then watch Him show up. This mindset gives Him the space to shine—not us. That is ultimately our goal, right?

We see this, at times, when God shows up and allows something monumental or significant to happen in our lives. As a response, we often say, "Only by God's grace did that ever happen." Sometimes it's the small moments that remind us we aren't in control. We can't control our learning experiences, but we can walk toward them while trusting they are doors opened by God. Within these learning experiences, we are praying for grace from our customers and clients, that we need forgiveness and patience as we learn from our failures as we go. But in turn, as we learn grace, we have to give *more* grace. All of it is accomplished by God's grace, which keeps us humble, grateful, and a little freer as we realize all things are through Him and by Him.

So, as you move forward to step into all your next opportunities and the open doors God is showing you, remember to have this expansion of grace for yourself as well. That you can rely fully on God's grace and all that He is developing in you, through you, and out of you. As a way to focus on what God's grace is and what living in grace and through grace means, I made a list of what relying on grace allows us to do.

Relying on God's grace frees me to make mistakes.
Relying on God's grace frees me to make decisions to move forward.
Relying on God's grace leads me to let go of the things He takes away.
Relying on God's grace allows room for the new in different seasons of my life.
Relying on God's grace frees me to accept my weaknesses.
Relying on God's grace frees me to accept blessings.

I needed to hear that last one because getting an unearned gift can be hard to receive. How about you? Do you accept freely given gifts well? A gift is the ultimate form of grace. Even if it was in the form of pizza, someone still gave me a gift and showed me kindness in the name of the Lord. I should accept the blessing with humility and gratitude. We have to get better at accepting it because that is what salvation is, a gift of grace!

The last "relying on God's grace" statement I want to remember is:
Relying on God's grace reminds me He's going to show up in all the ways I can't!
When I gave my friend the advice to "give God your best and He does the rest," I meant it as, *You don't have to be perfect, you try your best, give it to God, and ask Him to make something more from it—something more than what you are capable of.* When we live fully under His blessings and grace, we allow His favor to show up and make beautiful things happen. We get a bigger glimpse of

God in control of our lives rather than relying on ourselves. That's allowing room in your life for God to shine so you can say, "Not in my own ability but all glory to God by His grace."

Paul's point in 2 Corinthians 12:9 is Jesus gives you grace over your weaknesses so you can lean into God's strength. When you do, you feel more empowered to move forward in God's power.

Want to know if it all worked out for the florist to farrier story? After the journaling section, read how she continued to grow her confidence and became one of the top five farriers in the area. (That's out of over thirty farriers, just in case you were wondering.)

Reflection:

What part of this chapter helps you feel encouraged and free to take whatever step is ahead of you?

How will you apply the lessons to release the pressures of life or worries of feeling "not enough" or not "the best"?

What lessons have you already learned from your own life experiences that allow more thankfulness for where you are at this time in your life?

Think about what you have accomplished. Can you remember what God used in the failures you have already overcome?

Go ahead and write these notes to yourself. Set a reminder to pop up on your phone every day, at a time that works best for you (mine is at noon):

Give my best. God does the rest.

Not by my own abilities but for Him to shine.

In my weaknesses, He is strong.

What does that look like right at this moment? What weaknesses can you wear a little more comfortably, knowing He is using all of them for good?

For me, I'm still a work in progress. The statements of "relying on grace . . ." are all reminders to help me sink in what I am learning daily and sometimes even hourly! I have even thought of putting reminders of all the grace sentences on a wall, a mirror, or even putting them in the car. I know I need them over and over again! But overall, it settles my heart to keep giving my best, knowing fully all of the ways God will meet me to take care of the rest.

Going a little deeper now, do you know what you are good at? Has someone ever said, "You are really good at this!" But you still aren't moving forward in doing it. Why? Journal out why you aren't moving forward, then journal your questions and doubts and pray over them. Then DO what God says to do! Don't worry. This is a journey throughout the entire book. Keep going.

*If you need additional encouragement or help in your next steps, keep reading. God will get you there in His timing. If you ever need more guidance and sisterhood, I have designed a coaching program to go along with this book, because sometimes, God has to bring an outsider's view to really move you forward. Visit www.kendradeecarroll.com for further information.

The Backstory
Florist to Farrier

As you learn to jump forward on your journey, you need to know you won't see all of the steps at once. God wants you to lean on

Him as you take each step. With that, you need to realize it is okay if the road is hard to see and the big picture is still unknown. Sometimes, you aren't going to see exactly where you are going and how you are going to get there. And sometimes, the obstacles you encounter seem bigger than they truly are. It is going to be a part of the journey to just keep one foot in front of the other and trust God will guide and provide as needed.

When one student wanted to become a farrier, she had already done many other things; she was a basketball athlete, had a heart for the mission field, had gone to college, and was serving her family's wedding venue. As she was transitioning to becoming a farrier, she wasn't just worried about "not being good enough." She also had physical obstacles to overcome. But as the road and opportunities became clearer, the thing she did next is the most important takeaway because it was the part she could control. She spent time building her confidence!

I am so encouraged by how our friend went from living in doubt to being one of the top farriers in our county in two short years! I may not see the whole road ahead, and a road full of difficult challenges may arise, but if God plans it, and I walk in it, it will work out the way it *should.*

God opened the doors for her as He provided opportunities where she worked and rode alongside other farriers who taught her the skills and built her confidence as she started stepping out on her own. She worked a couple of days a week with others and a couple of days a week for herself for about six months until she got so busy, she was out on her own and rocking the new farrier world. Her client base grew from the recommendation of other farriers in the field, and God has been pouring blessings of provision and opportunities still today.

Everyone's story is different when it comes to building

confidence. My husband built his confidence by using the trial-and-error method of learning from his mistakes. He spent his start-up building confidence by gaining a community of clients to assist his growth and learning opportunities. He also continues to build confidence by seeking out places to learn, which furthers his education and knowledge. Sometimes that's a YouTube video or an in-person clinic. I have also seen how God has used circumstances where he has lost a client or something went terribly wrong to grow Dustin's knowledge. God grew him by allowing the failures and opportunities for my husband to seek out answers to why they happened. Finding those results helped him gain more confidence to continue to know how to better serve new clients and new situations. God's graciousness also never made the lessons too overwhelming. They always came one at a time to build lessons of slow growth that helped my husband learn best. The confidence continued to grow as God would bring new clients as he was losing others and the business kept balancing out. The pattern continued and confidence grew along the way.

For me to grow confidence, I go inward to a quiet place with God and try to develop the dream. I journal out the details and prayers. Then, I get a few friends that are willing to be guinea pigs and test it out. The more they love it, my confidence grows, and I want to share it with more people. The more I share it, the more excited I am to keep growing it. My confidence continues to build in the feedback I receive. I like to hear how to fix errors and visibly work them out. When I get to act out what I had dreamed up, watching what I imagined come to life, my heart takes flight and my confidence soars as I see the dream unfold. I get to a point where I want to share with the whole world what I have created or learned.

In the end, God knows the way you should go. He will guide you in who you are, the way you learn, and how you will grow. Your responsibility is to trust the open door and take the opportunity with obedience.

We should walk in confidence because we know in all things, God has gone before us, and He has the next step laid out before we even begin.

> *The LORD himself goes before you and will be with you;*
> *He will never leave you nor forsake you. Do not be afraid;*
> *do not be discouraged.*
> *Deuteronomy 31:8, NIV*

Chapter Two

To move forward in your calling, you are going to need to go back to better understand the next steps of where God is taking you.

Do you realize this calling is not a new direction from God? Can you look back on your life and recognize you have been following a path He has cleared for you all along? Take a minute to think about when this adventure really began. It didn't just happen because God is always developing something in us. He has been working behind the scenes. Maybe you've been practicing for it and you didn't even know it.

In this chapter, we will take a trip back in time to see how long God has been preparing you to use your talents and gifts. I know the feeling of being chased, nudged, pursued, and the mountain-chasing moments of God calling me to do something. So, I'm going to challenge you to seek out the answer to these questions: Do you feel called? Do you desire to explore parts of your heart that you may have silenced to know what it is you are being called to? You have to seek the prompting in your own heart that you can't ignore and know God is calling you.

The Call of the Heart

As another week passed into my new journey as a Bible-based business coach and writing this book, I wondered if I was really being called in a new direction or if it was a continuation of something God had already been working on within me. A friend told me God is the one who molds talents and encouraged me to look back as early as I could remember into my childhood to see where God had been preparing me for this journey all along. This reflection helped me believe in myself and gain the confidence to move forward. This reminded me to believe I was truly being *called.*

A man's heart plans his way, but the Lord directs his steps.
Proverbs 16:9, NKJV

The common phrase "call of the heart" could also be "call of the wild," because sometimes God's way is going to sound crazy or even unbelievable. It will often feel absurd to even consider. Nevertheless, you still have to jump! This call will nudge you and nag you; it will show you a need only you know how to fill. God will speak quietly to you, *"Here. Now. Do this."* Crack open the curiosity in your heart and explore! Allow yourself to join the journey God is calling you to.

It is helpful to take a step back to see how long God has been preparing the way He is taking you. You will also start to recognize all of the small steps that have led you to where you are right now and where you are going. When you do take a step back to see the bigger picture, you gain more confidence and assurance this is the right path. So, let's take a look. Where did this really all begin? I'm going to show you how I looked back in my own life to see what God was developing in hopes it helps you to do the same for your life.

For we are his workmanship, created in Christ Jesus for good works, which God prepared beforehand, that we should walk in them.
Ephesians 2:10, ESV

Ever since I was a kid, I have created things. One of my favorite childhood pastimes was making up performances to songs. I would take all day, putting on huge productions that included dancing and acting. Later in life, I put my love for dancing together with my love for horse riding and created a leadership and confidence program that utilized both skills. God allowed me to teach almost 400 students through that program. As I grew as a teacher in both leadership and confidence, I realized I had been a teacher at heart from a very early age. Being the oldest of five, I stepped into this role naturally as I led Sunday school classes at church, did a lot of babysitting, and worked in after-school programs. Wherever there was a need with kids I could fill, I was there! Because of my opportunities to be a leader at church, teaching the Bible began early for me. As I look back, I realize this was the turning point for two of the gifts God would have me use for the rest of my life: writing and teaching.

I was blessed with a Sunday school teacher who wanted us to practice journaling through the Bible, starting with Proverbs. I learned so much from the journaling process about letting the Bible speak to me in the silence. I practiced praying over verses until they really spoke to me, and I developed a way to share those journaling insights with my class. At the same time, while still only in fifth grade, I had the opportunity to start teaching a class of two and three-year-olds about Jesus. I was designing the crafts, learning games to play with them, and trying to help make Jesus and his stories real to them. I remember feeling the weight of the responsibility; I felt honored to just be used and serve my church. One memory that has always encouraged me was the day the children's ministry leader first called me and said, "Would you be willing to teach in the two and three-year-old class?" My response was immediate. I told her I was not only willing but I had been wanting and waiting to teach this class. This lady, with so much love and admiration for my faith-filled, child-like heart, responded, "Wow, Kendra, nobody ever says that, but that's exactly how God wants our hearts to be positioned." Because of that conversation, I held in my heart it was an honor to be a servant. This honor became a prayer I would always carry with me: to keep a waiting, wanting, and willing heart to serve however God would use me for all of my life.

> In all things I have shown you that by working hard in this way we must help the weak and remember the words of the Lord Jesus, how he himself said, "It is more blessed to give than to receive."
> Acts 20:35, ESV

Anyone who knows me well knows they can ask me to do *anything:* clean the bathrooms, sweep the parking lot, anything. If there is a need, I want to be used. I believe when we willingly fill a need, we embody the heart of the Lord to be a servant to all. I try to fulfill this in all aspects of my life: career, church, school, and my own family. As a mom, that heart can be overwhelming because I begin taking on all of the duties of everyone else. It became evident all of the ways I was sacrificing to help my children was failing them because it was keeping them from learning the value of a servant's heart in their own lives.

There can always be a downside to anything. Where there is a strength, there is also a weakness. I say all of this to remind you that you shouldn't shy away from using your gifts just because of a fear your weaknesses could get the best of you. Don't let the possibility of experiencing the downside keep you from prayerfully stepping into the *"more"* God has for you to discover.

As much as I love serving in all areas and fulfilling any need, I have come to realize if I have a passion and a love for doing what God has truly called me to, I find rejuvenation in my willingness and love for serving. What if you have the opportunity to align your talents, passions, and dreams and turn them into blessings for others?

For a long time, I prayed: "Lord, use me, my talents, and who you made me to be. Use all of me." Then, I would wait . . . and discover . . . and push for more!

As each has received a gift, use it to serve one another, as good stewards of God's varied grace.
1 Peter 4:10, ESV

I've worked with kids, horses, animals, music, and all of these in some combination. Yet, I know I have another talent that is underdeveloped: writing. It's something I have a hard time accepting. Perhaps it's because I don't know how to evaluate its worth. I often forget, for as far back as I can remember, God has been cultivating my skill and passion for writing. It's something I never thought God would really use in me. However, when we pause and gather all of our past experiences, we see what we have learned through every little lesson and opportunity. We can't miss the next step God has for us when we look back at the steps He's already provided for us.

If I hadn't looked back at my journey, I wouldn't have known I was called to write this book. I wouldn't have recognized this was the talent God wanted to develop and use more in me. Even in my personal journaling, I write as if, at some time, another person might read it one day. I write to stir the heart. I write to provoke enthusiasm and inspiration and to leave a path to guide others to learn from the insight God has shown me. As I evaluate who I am as a teacher and lover of Jesus, I take into account that God has let me practice teaching. Since I have mainly worked with kids, I've learned how to use imagery to build character, leadership, and confidence. I learned how to be honest and humble to gain trust. In my honored role as a teacher, I learned what demonstrating a deep love for others looks like. I learned, practiced, and implemented these principles in the horse program. Now, I feel called to express the same teaching style in this book, to love you and to lead you. We have to take all of the things God has allowed us to practice and apply them to the next step. Don't underestimate them, but take into account how they cross over. Horseback riding crossed over to writing a book, public speaking, and more in my life! What has God prepared *you* for?

Most people may look at my life and wonder, *Where is her next wild hair going to pop out?* and *What 'new thing' is Kendra going to try today?* But truthfully, these things have been inside me from the very beginning! I believe this is true for you, too. You have something already stored in you, ready to be used as a gift to others. Put aside what others might think when you try out your gifts and instead, build your confidence by focusing on who it might bless. As I write these words to you, my deeper reason to keep going is knowing that my reward is not for me but to bless and inspire you. My hope is this book will bless you so much, you will feel compelled to bless others as well. This is my example of obedience that I hope encourages you to do what you are called to do as well. I surrender all of these things: my calling, writing, talents, and all of my expectations to be used by God.

I know writing this book is not the final destination for me. One day, this moment and this project will count as a past experience too. After this, it will be time to dream bigger dreams, dreams that allow me to move forward beyond this book. I still dream of one day standing in front of thousands, raising people's spirits through song, speaking, and dance, all to share my love for Jesus. I want to host a party, not a show from the stage, but host a celebration of God, in unison as a family, with a heart drawn to love! It will be like throwing a dance party for Jesus with other believers. This dream reminds me that my sisters in Christ and I were created to encourage and support each other in our talents, dreams, and callings. It would be a beautiful reminder of what only He can do with how He made us as we serve Him wholly, fully, and excitedly to be all He called us to be!

Do not neglect to do good and to share what you have,
for such sacrifices are pleasing to God.
Hebrews 13:16, ESV

Our talents, gifts, and service are the best ways we can "do good" and "share what we have." However, this is not always tangible. Sometimes it's a good word or a song. Whatever God gives you, use it, give it, and share it. This will add to more of how God is building you to shine in everything you do; your business will become more about God's business and seeing God show up daily in your business will be a reward to the steps you are taking to align your dreams with God's preplanned dreams for you. See what happens when you surrender it to be fully His and ride the ride of Jesus' plan! For, His plans are always better than our plans when we let go and let God. By letting go, you can prepare your heart to see the amazing things He can do in your life.

I can't tell you how it will end because I just began this phase of the journey myself. But I know it's a journey worth taking because it's an answer of obedience to His calling and growing a deeper relationship with God, who wants us to trust in Him alone. Nothing else can save us or bless us the way He can. Let's work together to surrender all to Him, with our hands open and our hearts full—holding nothing back. I know I can't hold back what

I want God to bless. So, let's serve and say "yes" to the ways He is leading us.

Reflection:

Looking at all of your talents will help you see what other parts of who you are need to be put into what God is calling you to do.

Do you have a talent, even a hidden one, you never thought would be useful to God? What is it? It could be something you have enjoyed since you were young. Maybe it's a talent that only blesses your close friends, like finding creative ways to inspire kids to do chores. That's a blessing!

Have you practiced saying yes to God in other ways that have developed a skill or talent? What is that skill?

Look at ways you've already served in church or for a friend or even for an elder in your community.

If you haven't been saying yes to God, have you fully surrendered to His plan? Can you say, "I trust you God" at this moment? What areas of your life are still holding back from discovering or trying to keep control of?

Does walking in God's plan, of who He made you to be, excite you or scare you? In the areas where you feel fear, what would encourage you to change to excitement?
What steps do you need to surrender to trusting God from here?

Even the tiniest step can make a difference in your obedience to His call on your life. Go get started!

The Backstory
"Write a Book"

Truth be told, I argued with God about writing this book. I knew I was called to write a book, I just didn't want it to be *right now*. I wanted it to be at a slower time in my life, sometime after I turned fifty. At least, I wanted it to be at a time when I didn't have four kids I was trying to homeschool. I thought this was what I was asking for, negotiating with God for a *different* time. But God's timing always leaves us laughing, doesn't it?

I knew going through this process was going to rock me emotionally and spiritually. The other struggle is I feel like a hyper child in an adult body. Getting quiet enough to write a book was a constant fight. I had to learn to play mind games with myself. When this ranch girl was naturally outside before 8 a.m. dressed in jeans, I had to force myself to sit in pajamas at 11 a.m. to slow down. Everything in me, even right now as I write, wants to get up, get dressed, and move on to something else. But my heart says, "Be still. Write in honest, raw, real-time what it is like to fight for obedience over comfort and habits."

I knew the next steps God was taking me meant growing at a slower pace than I had ever done before. In the past, I built businesses on a Monday and was making money by Friday! This time, *oh this time,* I started my author/speaker/podcaster/coaching business nine months ago and still feel like there is so much more to create, so much more to get off the ground and running.
I had to sit in this feeling for months before the action of obedience; the feelings were preparing me for the change that was coming. At times, when I'm just walking around, I sense this awareness that this is bigger than me. I hear small whispers to "get ready to say yes," and "say yes in all the small ways, no matter what it looks like." My heart would stir like a secret recipe was being

made deep inside me. I would feel the pressure and the essence of how big this was, something so much bigger than me, something I knew I could only do with God if I stayed in His development and care. As I continued to prepare my heart for this 'yes,' I let the Lord continue to speak to my heart. These whispers ran over me like rain, watering me to help me grow.

Big dreamers know there are more dreams to achieve. They want the stars, they just don't always see the path to get there. Big dreamers take giant leaps of faith and sometimes miss all of the small steps in between. Other times, we fight the smallest, clearest answers because it looks too small to get us where we think we want to go. It makes me laugh that this fight is so true to me. I look for huge opportunities to move forward, but it is often just prayer, journaling, conversations with other people, or other God-ordained experiences that can help lead to the next right move in my life. God really works through even the smallest things, and we should not underestimate where baby steps can lead.

I was sitting in the third row from the stage of a gigantic church listening to Francis Chan when I heard the next step. My ears were open, as I had been praying for God to "give me ears to hear and eyes to see." I was being as intentional as I could to hear God as clearly as I could, knowing I had proclaimed two months earlier that I wanted to become a speaker. What I mean by proclaimed isn't anything fancier than meaning, I started talking about it. I took small steps by telling a few people in conversation that becoming a speaker was the way I wanted to go next. As I sat ready, willing, and waiting to hear inspiration from this amazing world-renowned speaker, I didn't get what I was expecting.

Francis Chan came out on stage and said, "I feel the Lord has not asked me to speak tonight. He has said I have fancy words and mastered my skill of speaking, and sometimes, I mess up His message. So tonight, I don't want to mess it up anymore. Tonight, I just want it to be God speaking." Then he set down his Bible, came to the middle of the stage, got on his knees, and went into silent prayer. In an auditorium of over 2,000 people, even five minutes of dead silence felt strange. There was no timer, but it felt like fifteen minutes of nothingness. All he said out loud were a few words: "God show up. Lead this"—and that was it.

I began to wonder: What was Francis Chan even doing? But what Francis did was set an example for what we all need to do—get quiet and be led by the Spirit. He prayed out loud for a few sentences, then he went right back to silence. This time, others knew he was creating a space for all of us to take time to hear God, and the silence for me became a moment to absorb the atmosphere and soak up any answers. As you will gather in this book, my prayers always begin with a question. So I asked, *What are you doing, GOD?!* This was the cry in my heart with a little fear because I had been sitting in preparation for God to do something *crazy*. I was so ready for crazy to happen, I could have jumped onto the stage right then. I thought, "Francis Chan needs rescuing because he ran out of stuff to say." I was *wrong*.

Francis was doing exactly what God wanted him to do and showing us how to get *quiet*. When he did speak, he would only read the last passage of the Scripture God gave him. He was setting an example of exactly what we are supposed to do: Go back to the last thing God told you to do, then wait patiently for the next. So, he reread the same verse, spoke from his heart, and prayed more.

In those quiet moments, I don't remember how the answer was pressed upon my heart, but it felt like it said, "Okay, if you are ready for all this, to be a speaker and have this much responsibility, go and write a book." I argued, of course, as we all have a tendency to do. "But God, my husband will not like me being an author. That will be a lot of sitting still, and it will frustrate him." When I came home to have a night chat with my husband, I didn't get what I expected. We began talking about business and other things, when my husband suddenly interrupted and blurted out, "You know what? I really feel like you are supposed to write a book." My mind froze! *No way, God, it's not this easy!*

I didn't tell my husband I felt the same way. I actually told him I was afraid he wouldn't be okay with me writing a book. I told him he didn't know what he was saying yes to or the unknown time it would take. I was right. He thought I could write a book in two weeks! I still laugh that he could ever believe this, but God knew what He was doing.

I woke up the next day, still not ready to write a book. I was feeling the task was too big and began to hope that maybe it was just a random thought to write a book, so I continued my routine of writing my Psalm devotionals instead. It was Psalm 135, verse 6 which talks about God doing what He pleases, knowing the depths of heaven, earth, and sea. These words started to stir my heart, and I heard God in this while I read it, "I tell you to do something, and you question me? Are you questioning what I know you are good at and what you asked for me to use?" Knowing God can give you anything, do anything, and make anything, I felt very humbled being affirmed God knows the depths of what He is asking. I needed to stop all that I was doubting and questioning.

Through time spent journaling, I began recording my doubts and concerns. After that, I called a Godly friend and asked them to help me push back the distracting thoughts, all of my doubts and concerns, and simply do *this*. This is when she asked me, "Well, tell me all the ways God has led you to this in your life *already*." She reminded me God doesn't throw things out of the blue that He hasn't already prepared for you all along. Through that conversation, I was led to write this chapter, and I continued to gather past experiences and see how God puts them all into play.

Doing this process of reflection not only gives clarity to the path, but it builds confidence and confirmation to go the way God has called you. So now, it's your turn to start seeing your past as a planted direction of where God has been taking you. Go back as far as you can remember where He has used you and prepared the lessons and training of what you are ready to do today. Were you five, eight, ten, or in your teens? Was it your first job or something even more insignificant, or is He bringing to mind that one conversation that really meant something? Use your past to gain the strength, encouragement, and courage to keep going forward.

As soon as I pray, You answer me; you encourage me by giving me strength.
Psalm 138:3, NLT

Chapter Three

After you start building in all of the necessary areas of your business or calling, it doesn't take long before managing life can feel overwhelming.

It's natural to desire to pull back or retreat from the feelings of being overwhelmed because we associate being overwhelmed with the opposite of peace. I was hitting a season where I was constantly overwhelmed. It was so consistent, I started to recognize it as a lesson, so I decided to ask God again, "Is this overwhelming feeling something You are using?" It made me wonder, do we stress ourselves out or does stress find us? If I'm overwhelmed, did I take on too much or is God stretching me to grow?

Overwhelmed or Growing Pains?

I've come to realize that every day we get stretched a little bit more into who God is calling us to be.

Whatever you have learned or received or heard from me,
or seen in me—put it into practice. And the God of peace
will be with you.
Philippians 4:9, NIV

The more I understand that God is training us every day for the tasks for which He created us, the more parallels I see to training a horse. A horse's natural response is to get scared and run away from what is overwhelming or intimidating them. In training, you have to help them fulfill the role for which they were created. The reality is, the only way to help a horse overcome what seems big and scary is to push them right into it. They have to learn to take it head-on until they are no longer afraid of it. Just as I train a horse, God is training me. Instead of running away from what seemed overwhelming, I needed to start to see God's hands training me for the growth of the next assignment.

A horse can fight and so can we, but when we embrace that God is using everything, we can surrender, knowing that wisdom and growth will come with the process. We can focus on the desire to know more about who God created us to be. We can choose to let God take us through the training and overcome the fears to reach the "more" He created us for. If we fight, God might back us into the lesson kicking and screaming. You should see a horse fighting a gate! But if you give in to the way God is leading, you will see all that you thought was overwhelming you is the blessing you were praying for.

If you read Philippians 4:9 (above), you can take things head on, a little less afraid, because you are putting into practice what God has taught you. When it comes to acting out of obedience to your calling, you can't get hung up on perfection. The action of obedience God is looking for is the yes. It's a yes with imperfections. It isn't based on how you are judging yourself to be perfect or even desiring perfection in a worldly way. We can't withhold our gifts of an imperfect cookie or song, for example, that could bless someone. A cookie still tastes good and sweet, even if it's not perfectly round. The thankfulness in the act of giving and receiving the cookie is all that matters. God desires the action of obedience and graces us to practice that obedience. Practicing doesn't mean perfect. Perfect is the obedience; practice is the gift. Practice is to see something new in front of you and keep trying at it until you get it right, remembering God is leading us through the practice. He is showing you the steps and holding your hand every step of the way. You have to decide to focus on walking in faith and the desire to be all God created you to be.

I guarantee the reason you feel overstretched and overwhelmed is because God is working on you. Even if you are stressed, He's working on you to do something different. If you seek to follow Him in all His ways that HE planned for you, then some of the stirrings you feel are Him waking that part of you that has been dormant. Just as we'd discussed in the last chapter, going backward gains confidence. We also have to go back to observe our own growth journeys and help us see all of the ways God is working in these growing and stretching moments!

I have a friend who was feeling overwhelmed. She is extremely knowledgeable about health, and every day she is flooded with questions from potential clients. She found that out of the average of eighty emails she receives daily, she could only respond to about thirty. Her messages were a mix of potential clients, existing clients, friends, and even family who were trying to check in on her. Unanswered messages left her friends feeling like they were slipping away, so she felt a heart tug to find time to give them attention. Moreover, she had a large family and worked to meet their demands. With all of this, becoming overwhelmed could happen very easily. But did all this happen overnight? Was she giving all of her time and attention in too many areas and offering too much of herself? Does too much mean she went wrong somewhere, or should she have learned how to balance it all before she got to this point? I don't think so. I think this grew over time, and what we have to realize is the growth wasn't meant to be overwhelming; the growth was the blessing. When she grew, she was not only growing a business that was becoming a bigger and bigger blessing, but God was stretching her human capacity into a blessing as she learned to lean into Him more. She could now bless others in a greater capacity because she was allowing more of God to be used through her. She had to change her outlook of feeling overwhelmed by these messages to see how many people God was allowing her to bless. She had to make a new system and a new way to serve through the growth He was bringing her.

> *"But the seed on good soil stands for those with a noble and good heart, who hear the word, retain it, and by persevering produce a crop."*
> *Luke 8:15, NIV*

God's growth isn't all overwhelming, and the pivoting position isn't as hard as it seems because God designed us to love the aspects of ourselves we were made to use. Whatever we love tends to grow naturally, especially if we make space and time for that growth. It happens naturally because we enjoy it. As we continue to learn more and seek the desires God has placed in our hearts, we continue to grow in using our gifts and talents for Him. Our desires and interests are fed, and we begin to grow in knowledge, understanding, and experience. This growth pattern continues and, as time passes, it's not long before we are eventually considered an expert in that area.

This friend had grown into the expert she had become; she once shared with me that she always wanted to seek out answers regarding health. She was intrigued, and one question led to another. Hours of research done over the years added up to a lot of knowledge. I'm sure she used this knowledge to benefit family and friends until the day she aligned her passion with her career. One day, that passion exploded into an ability to help others. Her business grew quickly, serving and helping hundreds in their own health journey.

*Teach me to do your will, for you are my God; may your
good spirit lead me on level ground.*
Psalm 143:10, NIV

Being overwhelmed can feel like something you brought on yourself. You start saying yes to too many things, things that were not your best "yes." Some of these "yesses" were to try to find where God might be calling you. Maybe your "yes" is even a fear of missing out on the growth and opportunities you have been seeking. Your "yes" starts to become a "do it all" mentality. This mentality tends to take flight and ends up taking away from growth. In fact, it can cause hurt in all aspects of your life. A heart that likes to say yes will fall into the trap of always wanting to "do it all." At least, I do. I can wake up with a list of three things to do on a particular day, then the next thing I know, I've added ten!

For example, I've been known to try to hit several parties in one day, just to make sure I'm not missing out or leaving someone feeling like I didn't show up for them. I will go to a baby shower at 10 a.m. Then, I would leave early to hit a birthday party by 1 p.m. Then, I leave again to go to dinner with my brother at 5 p.m. I could even be extreme enough to attend a 10 p.m. movie to double date on the same night, and somewhere in there, I probably offered to take extra kids along with me throughout the day as well. I tend to go to extremes, wanting to get it all in. But did God really call me to that? Am I really supposed to say "yes" to everything that comes my way?

The phrase "level ground" from Psalm 143:10, does not mean to go and run all the hills, taking all the paths, and not finding good direction with God as your guide. It's a reminder to walk with God, even mapping out your course. This Scripture asks us to walk the steady walk in front of us—focused, level-headed, and not overwhelmed.

When you have reached the point of feeling overwhelmed, you have choices on how to proceed. The choices are to push through full force, take off little bites at a time, or try something new. Pushing through can lead to a mentality that you just want to get this season over with. You want to hurry up and learn the lessons. The problem with the push-through method is you might continue to feel broken, a mess, totally out of control, scattered, and stressed. So, you might try the next option to take off little bites at a time. This is often the approach for many things and is most suggested in any large, overwhelming task. It's the method of watching that day's list get smaller and smaller. But if God is trying to speed up your pace or take you somewhere new, you have to make quiet space to learn the lesson. Make room to learn to listen and act on all of the instructions God has for you in this season. If you aren't making time to learn, you may miss out on the blessing. You might skip over what God has offered by choosing to neglect the growth or pace. So, you must come to realize when God might be teaching you something new. You have to allow the option for Him to teach you a new way of doing things. And that, my friend, takes a lot of courage that needs to be met with grace. We can go back to the beginning verse of this chapter and put the "something new" God is teaching us into practice.

I believe my friends' talent needs to be shared with the world. I believe she is walking in her calling, and I believe she is handling all of those questions and messages the best she knows how. But, she also knows God is still growing her. She has to find a way to continue to show up and deliver to who God brings her to bless. Whatever God gives you, put it into practice.

I love this concept! Once again, practice isn't perfect. But the Bible also says God is leading and guiding us always! We can say,

"Okay, God. I'm going to try to send out a message that will reach more of the masses at once. It's a little scary for me to try because I'm stepping out of my comfort zone. Moving from sharing with people one-on-one to the masses is a big jump. I'm stepping out to share the information I believe You have helped me understand so I may stay connected with others while sharing all You are doing for me."

To reach the masses, it might also mean getting a little more vulnerable with who we are and who we are becoming. For God to use us to the fullest capacity, we have to first accept the assignment and claim, "This is who I am for the world to see!" If we keep our blessings to ourselves and do not grow, we will miss reaching the people He has chosen for us.

We have to shine with Jesus in us! Whatever passions, desires, or love that is in our hearts, Philippians 4:9 says, whatever He gives us! And I believe to the fullest that "whatever" covers anything and everything. So, expand on whatever yours is, and shine and share it!

Don't sit in fear of "doing it wrong" because guess who is growing and guiding your practice? GOD IS! It's just another developing stage. Move forward in His peace. Let's look at that Bible verse again:

"Whatever you have learned or received or heard from me, or seen in me—put it into practice. And the God of peace will be with you."
Philippians 4:9, NIV

So "whatever" else He blessed us with, we are to share it not withhold it. I don't care if it's the bowl in your cupboard, the horse in the pasture, a meal, a story or a song, the art from your hands, or the words from your mouth, "whatever" is a broad word to remind you to use what you have. When we bless others with what He blessed us with, everyone gets the blessings and Jesus shines through. Let it grow however He wants to use it.

Don't be afraid to do what God is calling you to do because you want the reward of knowing you did what God asked and seeing Him continue to show up in your life and use you. There is a familiar story found in Matthew 25:14-30, the parable of the talents. The story is about a master who leaves his servants with some talents. He gave one servant five talents, another servant was given two talents, and the other servant only one talent. As we unpack the story, we begin to understand there was a reason for the starting amounts. We understand that the master decided to give the talents based on the amount of how much he trusted each of the servants. Two of the servants used their talents more wisely, and the servant who was trusted with one was afraid to do anything with his talent. But the servants who used their talents grew them, and in turn, were blessed with even more. So, whatever you have been gifted with, use it! Grow with what God has gifted you and repeat the cycle. Learn, share, grow, repeat!

Reflection:

In what ways can you now see God is training you to get to your assignment?

What is the assignment?

Think about some lessons you have already learned in life. Can you see some things that have been hard in your life that you can learn from and fix so you can move forward? What are they?

Do you know if you are called to serve larger numbers or in more intimate settings?

When you are learning a lesson, have you ever shared it with someone else to help them grow as well? Is there a lesson you can share with someone right now?

I happen to be someone who constantly asks, "Is this just a lesson for me, or should I share it with the whole world?" My heart's desire is to be someone who leaves an impact on everyone, whether I'm speaking with one or one hundred. But remaining careful of exactly what to share has taken prayer and spiritual growth to know when the timing is right. We each have our own struggles so taking them up with God is best. For me, it's a constant balance of learning the wisdom of what to share and what not to share.

So, it's your turn to ask: How will you put what you are learning into a message, sharing and allowing growth so Jesus can shine bright in you?

How can remembering that all of your gifts and talents are from God help take the spotlight off of you so you can use them and share more with others?

Look up the song "Start a Fire" by Unspoken. The beginning of that song talks about wanting to hide our talents from the world, afraid of being attacked by its cruelty and bitterness. We have to trust that the God who leads us to the "next level" prepares the hearts of those who need to hear it at the "next level." He has been preparing us all along! So, I pray for all of those who will hear my message even before I deliver it. I pray to use His words not mine, so no matter how many people hear the same message, it can be received on a personal level. I pray it resonates intimately and allows God to speak in every heart that hears it. I also pray my heart of loving others isn't lost when it answers multiple questions at once and that my vulnerability will show who I am and connect that love on a Christ-like level. And finally, I pray God is going to protect my words, as He knows my heart. So, I must trust Him as He uses my voice to be His vessel. I pray you will use these prayers over your life as well.

When you realize why God has you growing is not about you, it should make you a little braver to deliver whatever message or use whatever talent God has in your heart and take on all the lessons He is taking you through to help others along the way. All of this is still about Him! He who lets you learn it, wants you to share it! Go and be blessed in your talents, my friend.

The Backstory

Before I go on to tell you the story of the entrepreneur, I want to share the story of a mom. It was one of those particularly hard days. The toilet overflowed, the baby cut his finger grabbing something that should not have been in his reach, the toddler decided to see what a crayon tasted like and later puked it up in the car, and this mom still had to take the older sibling to a dance lesson.

Keeping a mindset that feels level-headed, like the verse about "level ground," can skyrocket and crumble all at the same time as a mom of multiple kids. The same thing can happen to anyone with multiple levels of responsibility, whether it's a job, house, or even volunteer related. But when I shared this idea that was on my heart, about how being stretched is God's growing pains preparing us for more of the blessings He has in store for us, this mom took a breath. She said, "Okay. I got this day. It's just practice. Practice in my attitude and responsibilities. God is going to help me through my faults and give gentle corrections, so I can fix not only what I have to put into practice today, but tomorrow's practice as well."

Even if we saw life more like practice for a dance recital, hundreds of hours of practice go into the year for three minutes of an on-stage performance. In life, it feels like God lets us have a hundred practice days, and the one moment He wants a bigger "yes," we need to realize it is something we have been well prepared for in advance. God's got this. So, my friend, take a breath. Stop living life like it is a performance, and remember, today is just *practice*.

Now, the Other Backstory
"Health and Wellness Coach"

My friend has an entrepreneurial heart. She and her husband run an in-person, service-based business on top of online health coaching. Knowing she has had years of practice as an entrepreneur to raise her to the next level, you can see how practice grows into more practice. The in-person service business stays very one-on-one. There is a maximum capacity of how many you can serve when you serve one-on-one versus the online product that has more room for growth; sharing a message online to a bigger audience leads to endless possibilities because there is not a "max" number in place. It becomes limitless. Her message of wellness can be broadened.

I think when we are comfortable with one way of doing something, it can be extremely hard to break through to that next step without some guidance or outside awareness. When you can be aware of the changes God is taking you through, it is easier to recognize the need for a new approach. My friend didn't want to lose that personal touch from the in-person experience, but she was missing people altogether! She had a choice to completely abandon some customers or loosen her idea of the one-on-one personal connection. By creating videos to broaden her reach, she was able to be personal and share information without leaving anyone out.

This friend is also particularly private, so stepping out of her comfort zone to do this was a huge stretch. Now, I see her growing, opening up more about her family, business, and God on social media. By allowing God to stretch her in this new way, she's been able to lessen the messages that were overwhelming her. All of those people who used to just check in on her, now, get to see her, support her, and love on her in that new way. Utilizing these new tactics continued to stretch and grow her, allowing her to become more vulnerable while sharing her personal and business stories.

I know some people have no problem talking to a small group, getting up in front of a crowd, or even having deep one-on-one conversations, telling their whole story. But it can get pretty uncomfortable to do that video thing. It's harder, and it is completely different, especially if you are a people person because recording feels impersonal. It might feel like that because facial reactions are missing on the other side. It's also harder to learn how to answer or ask questions when it's not in real time. It feels uncomfortable to not make personal contact when you can't give the hugs you feel one may need.

Growing and getting out of your comfort zone means learning to do everything differently. When God stretches you, you may find yourself in a place where you really don't know who you are serving. Some people might stop in and see your social media post, website, blog, video, or podcast, and you will never know they did. If you are getting stretched to grow in an online platform, it is sure to leave part of who you are out of the bigger picture. This can cause a fear that part of you is being missed because it's a smaller snapshot than an in-person conversation offers. It's frustrating and uncomfortable, and I get it! But the more we give in to the new ways God is offering the opportunities to grow through, the more we see how He really can use it. The more we embrace where He is leading, the more people we can touch. The more people we touch, the more they, too, can grow in His kingdom. All of this happens when we decide to not stay comfortable. All of this is because we sought to understand there is a new way God is using and growing us.

If this friend can make videos and get outside her comfort zone, so can you! Whatever your comfort zone, God is trying to break barriers and help you overcome them. I promise the *blessing* of staying in Godly obedience, in His favor, and knowing you're doing His will, will comfort your heart as if you are walking hand in hand with God in the garden of Eden. Your development He has been walking you through reassures you that He will use you. Knowing He is right next to you will motivate you to push through this growth. As you grow, you will find more ways to get in front of the audience that needs you personally, professionally, and genuinely—in person, on paper, in audio, or on camera. Maybe it's even expanding your business or going international. Whatever God is calling for your next step, don't let your comfort zone stop you!

See, I am doing a new thing! Now it springs up; do you not perceive it? I am making a way in the wilderness and streams in the wasteland.
Isaiah 43:19, ESV

Chapter Four

There are going to be moments in your life when you are going to need to do something bold for your faith. It's important to address this before it comes.

Does being bold mean the same thing as being harsh? Is boldness something that will offend others? Doesn't the Bible say to "be bold"? The answers are no, sometimes, and yes. You don't have to be harsh in your boldness, but, yes, sometimes people will be offended if you are bold. And finally, yes, the Bible does say to be bold! I believe boldness has been misunderstood because of other interpretations and feelings. We sometimes get confused about what it means to be bold and how to use it as a gift.

Be Bold

The wicked flee when no one pursues, but the righteous
are bold as a lion.
Proverbs 28:1, ESV

I recently posted a picture from Narnia with Aslan, the lion, and Lucy, a daughter of Eve. They are standing side by side on a mountaintop, overlooking the land. The photo is a great visual reminder of the confidence we carry by having the Lion with us. It's a reminder that God, our lion, walks by our side. He is the one who helps us, defends us, and guides us. Oh, the confidence we can feel when we remember God is there, as well. If we can always hold the reminder in our hearts that God is with us in all circumstances, we would remain confident, building bravery, trust, and assurance to obey whatever God is asking us to do. But how often are we tapping into that Lion? Are you really walking in bold confidence? Are you feeling fully covered in God's love, remembering who you belong to before you go into the battles of the day?

Do you wake up and speak life to all the reminders in the Bible that encourage you to be strong and bold? Do you soak in God's love to remind yourself how loved you are? Do you drench yourself in God's goodness so much that you can get through the day, say what needs to be said, and cover it with grace and assurance?

Most mornings, I remember to stand in all God's truths when no attacks have had a chance to happen yet, but in a world like ours— full of division and hurt—the things we try to speak with boldness and bravery that Jesus places on our hearts can be trampled upon quickly. It's a reminder of how much grace it really takes to get through the day and exercise this boldness.

A few weeks ago, I was completely misunderstood when trying to encourage someone, even though, in my heart, my intentions were good.

I have always made it my goal to have tough conversations and to seek more understanding from people with other perspectives and opinions. These conversations help me exercise grace, while I keep in mind we are all God's children. I press in to more grace as I realize those I might disagree with also have the Lion standing beside them as well. If we are in an argument, I see the Lion is going to play dad and say, "You are both right, and you're both wrong." When God, our Heavenly Father, the Lion, is Father to both of us, we need to speak God's truth in boldness rather than earthly opinions. So, we must learn the lessons in boldness and grace to be able to communicate even about difficult topics. Christians are being a light to the world when they can speak with compassion, bold authority, and fearless love over a topic of hate but still declare God's truths.

I was encouraging a friend on one of her social media posts to continue to share boldly. My comment read like this: "Yes, friend, be bold and brave and say what you need to say." Someone replied to my comment, "With gentleness and grace, a harsh word will not be heard!" *What!?* I thought to myself, as I reread what I said. I had used the words "bravery and boldness" but nothing about harshness! Did I sound harsh? I questioned how my words were being interpreted. I re-read them, still perplexed. I read them ten times, trying to see them from every angle, including reading other comments. I determined that, no, I did not say something harsh, and I could find nothing that hinted at harshness.

The thing was, my friend I was trying to encourage is one of the most gentle, meek, and sweet speakers ever! That is why I encouraged her in the first place. I wanted her to have bold confidence to go for her goals, be herself, and share what God has been teaching her. Her topic of the post was about standing in what you believe but showing grace, so I wanted to add where grace meets boldness because God was taking her there. But, it didn't take long before someone was triggered enough to quickly tear down my words of encouragement to her to "be bold and brave." And, I was more shocked that it was a Christian whom I would have referred to for representing boldness in her own ways. I had to step back a moment and wonder, *Am I wrong to encourage someone this way? Why was it received as a warning instead of the high-five of encouragement I meant for it to be?*

After returning to my Bible to look up all of the verses on boldness and confidence for more understanding, I came away believing there is an epidemic of misunderstanding boldness among American Christians. We cower down to people's opinions, while in other countries, they confess with their lips, willing to be put to death. We worry about losing friends, jobs, and maybe even stature if we confess God too boldly here in America. So now, it's my turn to speak frankly about this. I think a lot of Christians are too timid. And being too timid has led to them not speaking the truth at all. It is sad to see so many have completely lost the meaning of "confidence in Christ." Many people think we can't have tough conversations where we disagree, even on Biblical topics, and still show love. The answer is yes, we can! We can say difficult things in love, and it can be done with grace. You bet!

Should it not be said at all? Maybe. It all has to do with discernment. It requires practice to consistently listen to the Holy Spirit, to know whether or not it is the right time for that person to hear it. Be extra sensitive to this if you're having an individual, one-on-one conversation.

So, what if you are speaking to the masses? What if you are just boldly sharing something that is on your heart? What if it is not up to you how another perceives it? In public, bold statements will often mean something to one person, it doesn't have to be the whole group. Even though my comment encouraging my friend to "be bold" felt attacked, I wasn't talking to the one who responded to me. So, I believe God was working in the situation, and my encouragement was obedience. I did try to reach out for clarification and a better understanding of why this was off-putting to the lady, but I'm still unsure, as she didn't want to talk about it. But, what if you are talking about yourself and you hurt someone's feelings? It is at these times we have to remember God is working in that person; that wasn't all you. If your words are from God, you are to share them with bold confidence. I say that as a direction. Just like Joshua 1:9, NIV, says, "Be strong and courageous. Do not be afraid." This was the order given to follow through with what the Lord had said. The rest is up to God and how He uses it.

Have I not commanded you? Be strong and courageous. Do not be afraid; do not be discouraged, for the Lord your God will be with you wherever you go.
Joshua 1:9, NIV

Now, please know, I'm not giving you permission to just shout out your political views or opinions willy-nilly while claiming, "The Lion's got my back."

The bold words come from thoughts that are centered on love and focused on *Jesus.* They hit when you are coming out of your prayers and conversations with God. You carry them with the burden God has placed on your heart and feel convicted to be bold about the things He has been teaching you. It's these words I encourage you to speak and share boldly. They are to help others learn the truth and to see God working in us. They are pure and good words from the Father when your heart's desire is that your boldness brings new understanding and perspective to the glory of God.

The Bible says, "bold as a lion" from our key verse found in Psalm 28:1.
The lion walks around, unworried about "hurting someone's feelings." He is completely oblivious to his attackers because he's on top of the food chain.

If you are second-guessing everything God puts on your heart to say because you are worried about who is going to take it the wrong way or who is coming back at you about it, you're not being bold like a lion, as Psalm 28:1 calls us to be. You are wishy-washy in your mind and not walking in wisdom and confidence.

But let him ask in faith, with no doubting, for the one who doubts is like a wave of the sea that is driven and tossed by the wind. For that person must not suppose that he will receive anything from the Lord; he is a double-minded man, unstable in all his ways.
James 1:6-8, ESV

This verse really shows the opposite of "bold," and lacking the confidence to follow through makes us "unstable in all our ways." It is not going to build a voice of truth within us. We *must* follow through with our God-given assignments and messages. Hear my deeper, serious commanding voice tell you in the authority of Jesus Christ, "Say what you need to say!" I'm not telling you to say whatever you feel, no matter who it hurts. No, we must remember God cares about relationship building and doesn't want us to act out of our own pride. I am saying that if God says to talk about something, you do just that. You stick to saying what God wants you to say. You share the lessons you are personally learning, and even if you find out someone disagrees, or what you said hurt their feelings, you trust in what God is having you say. In moments where they attack your words, mistaking it as a personal affront to them, remember that God stirs the heart. Words are God's seeds of His timing for perhaps future conversations, and He will lead the conversation as you allow. Any arguments or misunderstandings were not actually your doing at all if you are saying what God wants you to say. Don't let that stop you from sharing again. Instead, stop and pray for the heart that was stirred by God. Then, without fixing it yourself, leave it with God. There is nothing else you can do about that. Only God can finish what He started. It is not our place to pursue another's lesson.

If we apologize for where God is working, even if we say, "I think you should pray about that more," we have inserted ourselves. We did not leave room for others to decide to question God more, and we didn't allow God to do His work. We made the fight about us, rather than allowing God to move! Don't seek them out to apologize or even to tell them to pray. It is not going to fix matters; it will make them worse. It is not our business. It is out of our jurisdiction. We said our part. That was our *obedience*.

Guys, I say this because I'm struggling, and in these situations, I want to apologize. I want to work it out. I want to have pretty conversational packages that end up nice, neat, and wrapped in bows. But I can't. The reality is, this happens a lot. Others get stirred by what I say because I share so freely. I have had people say, "Wow, Kendra, ouch! You are speaking right at me." Once, I was able to respond, "I'm sorry. I'm just talking more for me and about me." This conversation was with a wise woman who knew where she was with God, and she answered, "No, no. I know it's God using your words. They are just literally meaning a lot right now. I can't even explain. It's good; it's just coming on strong, and God must know what I needed to hear from you. Keep going girl. You're preaching it!" Luckily, that was only a one-on-one conversation, so we were able to chat it out, but it doesn't always look that way.

I recently had to do some business "clean up" with someone I invited on to my team. I realized some things weren't sitting well with how this person was operating in the business, and I heard God say, "Go clean that up. It's becoming a weed." I was feeling the nudge to handle it now or it would be a mess if I didn't straighten it out immediately. I recognized the prompting of God asking me to do it now, in His timing, as an immediate call to obedience. I asked for prayers over the conversation before going to address this person because I knew that my boldness in straightening the issue could lead to misunderstanding. The goal of the conversation was "do you want in or out" of the business, but I wanted to leave it on good terms, not harsh ones. I was also going to have to address what was going wrong, and this was where it was up to God to fix her actions, not me. God was going to have to help her choose if this was the right business team for her. Whenever I go into these situations, I remember the story of Esther chapter four, where she needed bold prayers from her people to help her with confidence and bravery to boldly approach the king. So, every time I know God is leading me to a "be bold" moment, I seek out prayer over my words from others first.

I see God use me most when I speak from my own experiences, my own desire for more of Jesus, and my own situations of what's not been enough for me. I share from bold honesty of where I am, who God is to me, and how He is working in me. These are the stories I'm giving you right now. These are my stories, and they are the stories of my friends who have needed me to be bold as well. But, overall, the stories are of times when I needed to uplift someone else, and in turn, I left more inspired and encouraged to keep going on the path God has before me as well. You must start believing your story can help others. Share it *boldly*. Share with confidence what God has taught you and what He is doing in your life. You never know how it will inspire others and come back to inspire you again.

...proclaiming the kingdom of God and teaching about the Lord Jesus Christ with all boldness and without hindrance.
Acts 28:31, ESV

To me, boldness accompanies authenticity and honesty. If people know that, they will recognize it and become bolder and more honest. Unfortunately, our world is lacking so many authentic, bold, honest characteristics that people are taken back when they are met with this combination of boldness. I find many people even question the authenticity around them even more! They seem to wonder if bold people still have "other motives"? People have done this to me countless times. They wonder, "Why her?", "Why so much confidence?", or "Who gave her authority?" I've even heard that I scare people with my boldness, despite my desire to be approachable and kind. Those who know me or reach out find I am super reachable. Through the process of seeking out different conversations, it has been a good growing tool to become more welcoming, allowing opportunities for good conversations with people from all sides. I find more grace when I get to see the other side of the table, and I've learned it takes a bold person to go look for it. I seek out an opportunity of opposing views, not for the debate, but for the understanding. And through that process, I've not only learned to love the conversation but love the person for whom God has made them as well.

I have a friend who I know stands totally opposite to me in most views, except Jesus. But, because of our relationship and love for each other as friends, I have learned to ask the right questions to find out why we have such different views. I will ask questions from every angle not to sound undermining, but in a way that says, "I want to learn" and have conversations until I understand her side to the fullest. These conversations are not to change anyone's views, although perhaps they can, but it's more for understanding. I just understand why she believes what she believes. When I understand why, I have more *grace and understanding* to offer anyone that may see it the same way she does. Not everyone will be okay with these types of conversations; it takes having a relationship first, one that starts and ends with love and appreciation for each other's differences. She helps me better prepare myself and my responses to make sure I'm leaving grace to the other side that I might not have seen before our conversation.

*But in your hearts honor Christ the Lord as holy, always
being prepared to make a defense to anyone who asks you
for a reason for the hope that is in you, yet do it with
gentleness and respect.*
1 Peter 3:15, ESV

Often in this world, it is hard to determine right and wrong or even good people or bad people. So much of this is because of how we perceive it. Therefore, only Biblical issues and Biblical truths hold water, and opinions have to remain *respectful* of feelings for discussion and different interpretations.

Taking that first footstep in my search for "common ground" in a very split and divided world took boldness. However, I knew that even when I was asking the tough questions, I could still come out with love and respect for my friend, no matter how opposite she is to my thinking. Why? Because God holds her heart and my heart! If we are both seeking truth, no matter how the road looks for us to get there, I trust God will lead both of us to the truth in the end. I'm not in charge of my friend's journey–only God is. Too often, we are trying to play Jesus and save everyone. We're striving to forgive everyone and help them heal from their sins, wrong ways, or wrong views. That's not our job. We did not take their burden on the cross, and we do not see their heart. Our job is to love gracefully and speak boldly.

*And also for me, that words may be given to me in opening
my mouth boldly to proclaim the mystery of the gospel.*
Ephesians 6:19, ESV

It is not an easy job to "open our mouths boldly."

The idea of just opening my mouth, speaking, and hoping God

takes the words scares me, especially because the first verse that pops into my head warns me how terrible my mouth can be when it is not controlled. It's scary to know that without caution to our boldness, our tongues can be twisted and speak in deceit.

The tongue also is a fire, a world of evil among the parts of the body. It corrupts the whole body, sets the whole course of one's life on fire, and is itself set on fire by hell.
James 3:6, NIV

I'm fully aware I have to move forward prayerfully and gracefully. I know the amount of grace I'm going to need to be offered back to me as I grow into a speaker. I will need grace for the misspoken, out-of-turn, or misconstrued words that might happen as I step forward. I will need the grace to stretch this tool—my mouth—to be used by God and for God. I need to ask, "Give me grace in Jesus' name!" If we all exercise grace, then we can all practice more boldness and step forward in commanded confidence to share what God has placed on our hearts. He has given an assigned message to share with urgency and truth.

We must also act in boldness with our talents and gifts. We can't let the enemy shut us down from serving others in a way that brings blessing to our hearts and others. In a Hebrew word search on bold, I found the words "heroic" and "audacious." I thought about how much I shrink back when I feel bad about my gifts or hear the enemy whisper, "What good will that do?" It can hinder me so much that I don't take that step of obedience. Or he whispers, "What you have is not that special," so I don't try to share it. "Are you really helping anyone anyways?" and then, I slow my roll and don't help the next one because the enemy has convinced me I'm useless. These lies can surface in your own head, or the enemy can use others to stir your doubt about who you are and who God has called you to be. I thought about how the enemy boxes you in and makes you feel small, and this creates a helpless victimized feeling of worthlessness. That feeling of uselessness is the complete opposite of heroism. The narrative of worthlessness is the opposite of audacious authority as a child of God. Luckily, when we find ourselves shrinking to these accusations, we have Jesus, our rescuer, to lean into. He restores our bravery and boldness so we can use our gifts in heroic measures, in the name of Jesus Christ. He restores us so we can help others meet their Rescuer through the ways we were created to serve them.

I started thinking deeper about how, when we use our gifts boldly for God, He puts us in heroic situations where we can meet the needs of others and be Jesus' hands and feet here on earth! This is also helping me see how to encourage you to not be shy with your gifts but offer yourself abundantly, so others will see Jesus in your gifts and feel loved through your service!

I see now why bosses tend to see themselves as heroic, giving out paychecks and taking care of others. But it can be a conceited trap if not done through the thankfulness of the Lord's blessings and redirecting the focus back to Him!

But my friends, everything you do is for the Lord! Every breath you breathe is to serve the Lord!

So, reach out and love on someone heroically, boldly, and confidently, so they might be rescued in Christ's name! And be sure to tell the enemy, "Get behind me, Satan!" Because you have audacious authority to serve others you are called to serve in the name of the Lord, the way He created and intended for you!

Be bold in your character as you serve in your calling. You will need it for your perseverance to stay focused and firm in your direction, determined to be all God is calling you to be remaining uncompromising on the promises and service He has called you to.

Reflection:

If the wicked are always fleeing, what are you fleeing from? What do you always find yourself questioning, doubting, and hiding from being bold?

Boldness comes with a position of awareness that nothing but God matters. We are here to please God, not man. Are you serving God or man in your actions and conversations? Explain.

Do you think you will be bold enough to have real conversations? Do you trust yourself to cover the conversation in love? Think about who you have loving conversations with and who you have hard conversations with, and then pray for the person and over your next conversation, to see God move more in love, grace, and understanding.

Knowing you are loved is a good way to stay centered in walking in boldness. Being loved by God means you know you are completely cared for as His child. Are you walking in love right now? Do you feel completely cared for? Name the characteristics of God that help you feel loved.

In what way are you boldly serving others with your gifts and taking bold authority to activate Jesus in you as you serve?

I hope you are like me, and now, you can breathe again after going through that hard topic. I worried, in the beginning, how misunderstood this chapter might be, as I explained the difference between "now is the time to be bold" versus "now is a time to not speak," and I realize the Holy Spirit will still have to help us with that. Always remember to give grace to yourself as you practice boldness and remind yourself and others to "be bold." It may ruffle feathers, but keep in mind Joshua 1:9. God says, "Have I not commanded you? Be strong and courageous. Do not be afraid; do not be discouraged, for the Lord your God will be with you wherever you go" (NIV). "Wherever you go" means He is with you, even on the job, on the Internet, with friends, in a coffee shop, and in every conversation. Even there, God is with you. Regroup your confidence and try again. Get bold. Be *bolder*. Get brave. Be *braver*. Those are the words I've felt God working on in my heart as I step forward in obedience. I am working to become who He is calling me to be, and I am encouraging you to do the same as well. Be bold and brave, my friend. You are covered in *His* love. If you work to be honest and full of truth, that is being bold and brave. We can do this!

Look up more verses with these keywords: bold, confident, unwavering, indecisive, and see what God stirs in your heart, and journal it.

Backstory

I'm going to share a story of boldness in business, something my friend said felt like an "Esther moment" to her. God had asked her to start this business; God had given her the dream, the vision, the location, and all of the details of the building. Her story of building this business with the Lord is one of seeing God's miracles as He walked hand-in-hand, opening doors and paving the way. Beautiful details in this cafe, from the location, the big windows on the street, to the flowers on the walls, were just a Holy Spirit breathing all over her business.

Now, she was much like any of us; she, at first, argued with God about even doing business. But then, He gave her more purpose with the business and had her open a cafe where the extra proceeds would support pregnancy care centers in Ukraine. These centers are houses for women who are pregnant, have been abandoned, and need extra support. Knowing the purpose God had for the business helped build her heart to be all in for her "yes" to serve God and start the business. Then, God started building the little, beautiful details of the business, and this made her fall in love with what God was calling her to do. But, it didn't take long before God asked her to make another step of boldness that she believed was going to end her business, after faithfully building for only eighteen months. The steps of obedient boldness felt too hard. She didn't want to do it; she couldn't find it in herself to do it, but she knew the Lord was calling her to it.

It was the week the war broke out between Russia and Ukraine. She is Ukrainian, and her business serves mainly Russians here on American soil. The Lord asked her to put out a box on the counter that read: "Pray for Ukraine" and to collect donations. She thought, *Surely I will upset and offend everyone, and I will have no more customers ever again.* She cried tears and called out to God, "Why, God, do you want to take this away? Why do you ask so many hard things of me? I was obedient in building this, now you want to take it from me. Why!?" It felt like an Abraham and Issac sacrificial moment mixed with an Esther signing up for a death sentence, but instead of her life, it was her business.

She begged God to ask someone else to be this BOLD. It took her three days of prayer to muster up enough courage to put out the box. She came to the conclusion that if God led her to this business and all she does is for Him, then she must do this too. She was heart-wrenched and drained going through the emotions. Even after placing the box on the counter for all to see, she told her workers, "This is too heavy for my heart, I have to go home." This was at around 10 a.m. on a Saturday morning. At 5 p.m., she received a phone call from a faithful customer announcing they noticed the box for Ukraine and called the local news station.

Shocked and terrified, my friend responded, "Why did you do that? I don't want ANYONE to know about that box." The voice on the other end tried to encourage her; this was a good thing, and in bold confidence, told her, too bad if you're nervous, because the news crew will be at your shop to film you and your story at 9 a.m. tomorrow morning.

You might have known as I did, this story has an AMAZING turnaround. But you have to remember my friend's emotions. What the Devil was whispering to keep her afraid and hiding, not speaking and not showing up, was a real spiritual battle, and she fully believed she was facing the death of her business. BUT, God showed up! She got on camera, chose boldness, told the story God had placed on her heart, and that the money she was collecting for Ukraine was to help take food, water, and supplies from western Ukraine to eastern Ukraine.

They were closed the day after the interview, and the following business day was normally a slow day. A typical day would be forty cups of coffee on average, but that morning, they served 142 cups of just coffee, not counting any other purchases. The rest of the week, the business grew and grew. By the end of two weeks, she had collected four thousand dollars and was able to buy two trucks of supplies to support the Ukrainians. This story is to encourage you to remain bold in all your "yesses," because when God gets ahold of our "yes," amazing things can and will happen.

The other area we must continue to be bold is simply sharing our faith. I have practiced boldness often in my life. I remember one time, about ten years ago, I saw a homeless man in front of McDonald's, and I felt God urge me to go talk to him. I had my three-year-old daughter and four-year-old son with me at the time, and zero money to give this man, so I questioned what to even say. I felt I was being asked to walk up to this man and say, "Jesus loves you." Sounds pretty simple, right? I had many doubts running through my mind: *But what if he gets angry?* I thought. *He is sitting here, with nothing. How is he going to believe Jesus loves him?* I swallowed hard and walked toward the man in obedience. I bent down to the man who had his head down and said, "I'm sorry. I have nothing to offer you, but I feel like I'm supposed to tell you Jesus loves you."

He looked up at me and said, "Thank you. I've been thinking about that. I was wondering if He did. You see, today this man gave me new shoes, and I felt like it was Jesus' love for me, but I don't think I deserve God's love." My heart was so touched that God was here in this conversation and showed me I didn't have to have something in my hands to give in order to obey God. I just needed to be obedient to what He was saying, *You never see the big picture until you obey.* This was a simple way to share God's love, and I got to see how God brought new shoes and was showing up in miraculous ways. If you want to see God working more in your life and the lives of others, act in boldness.

Right then and there, I had the opportunity to extend God's love, to remind this man we are never too far from His grace and His love. It is always available to us, and the thing is, none of us deserve it. After we had finished our conversation, my children and I prayed over this man and gave him a hug. He thanked us for showing God's love to him that day and said it was just what he needed. It was a turning point for him because he knew now, with confidence, God loved him. He felt now he had permission to seek God and His goodness in his life again.

For me, it felt like an amazing moment to share with my children. It was a chance to put God's love into action with nothing but words. It felt like a Peter and John moment, as in Acts 3:6 when they didn't give money to the lame man but healed him instead. I didn't send a lame man walking, but God did use me to help Him set a heart free and give a man a chance for new life. For those of you who are skeptics of the homeless (because I've even become more cynical myself), it's still important to remember to move when prompted, no matter who it is. We never *know* what God is going to do through us if we are willing. I never did see this man again. Perhaps this was the day he was set free and changed his ways. However, that's all up to God, not me. When we walk in doing God's will, we don't question the outcome because we truly know it was God. But what if I had disobeyed? What if I hadn't said what was on my heart out of fear? I could have easily feared what he could have done to me or my children. I have always taught my children to talk boldly to strangers, but my initial fears asked me, "What if he is angry?" However, all I could think about was how I would prove God's love to this man. Walking in confidence in Christ means I know I can't prove anything; God does that part. God had this man's heart ready for this message, and my blessing was from the obedience of being used for God's glory. I'm so glad I chose to walk with the Lion that day. It's the little moments like these that have led me to the bigger moments of obedience—moments where I thought, "Say it anyway," as bold as a lion.

Chapter Five

When you are serving others, there is a level of professionalism and a level of care that needs to be authentic, no matter what. Your life should revolve around caring for others, and we need to do it in a way that best shines Jesus. We must learn to be a truly authentic version of ourselves to reach others where they are at.

In a world where most people aren't willing to show raw emotions, feelings, and a true version of themselves, how will we embrace this idea of fully being who we are? Too often, we only want to show the best of ourselves and the rest of us can hide in a closet. So, how can we be authentic and embrace the whole realness of who we are? Better yet, when will we realize God needs us to be this way: fully, wholly, and truly ourselves?

Authentically Raw

Search me, O God, and know my heart! Try me and know my thoughts! And see if there be any grievous way in me, and lead me in the way everlasting!
Psalm 139:23-24, ESV

Be all you! Tears, emotions, joy, silliness, straightforwardness . . . whatever! The way you would talk to your best friend should be the way you talk with Jesus and the community He placed around you.

Before you can learn to share in a vulnerably authentic way with others, you first have to be all real with God. If you can't be real with Jesus, the one who died for you and loved you first, then who can you be real with? If you can't pray authentically to God who made you, who created all your emotions and personality, and who knows you better than you know yourself, then who can you be authentic to? If you can't be real with God and Jesus—you can't truly be yourself for anyone else either. It all starts with God first. So, even if the prayer is hard, or the emotions are more than you want to handle, the best thing you can do is practice owning it and laying that at the feet of Jesus.

If I am being honest, it took a few years for me to be okay with crying in church. I did this because of how I thought other people perceived it: "You crazy person! Hold it together. This is church!" Now, I wish I could take it back, because sometimes, the emotions can come on so strong. I just want to tell those people who wish church looked pretty and put together all of the time that church is a part of my quiet time to meet God. Church shouldn't be about flashy lights, set structures, and always the right thing to say, but more of a place to meet and commune with God our Father. It should be a quiet space of refuge and a place to rejoice in what God is doing; a place to hear from God, reflect, rejuvenate and reconnect. I think we still have some stripping to do to get it back to the "house of prayer." When I walk into church, I'm intentional about listening for God between the songs, the greetings, and the words spoken. I posture my heart, not focused on all that is around me, but to be so in tune to say, "Lord, I'm listening and here for you and you alone." Because church is God's house, He's going to show up, and sometimes speak personally and directly to us. Our job is to come in open and ready to receive. When we receive a word from God, we might be emotional, and that's okay! For me, sometimes I'm going to get a little heart-wrenched. And sometimes, those emotions are gonna show on my face! I've gotten to a place to be so unashamed of my emotions, that my heart's desire is pure worship, *let me be heart-wrenched God, let me be all yours and completely captivated.* And then, I start praying for others to catch the presence of the Holy Spirit, to be whispered to, held, comforted, or even danced with.

Preparing a heart postured to hear from God also needs to be in our daily lives. In our busy lives running here and there, we forget to leave time for the quiet. We don't leave enough space to get to hear from God as much as we truly need. We need to seize every opportunity we can—to take a moment to lock the doors while we're getting dressed in the morning and hit our knees. Bathroom breaks are often my Jesus moments. I don't leave until we have checked into that alone space. Every mom knows the bathroom ("one more minute") trick. And if I'm driving with nothing else to focus on, God's talking in my thoughts. All little moments can be God's moment. These are the moments to pray over the directions God is taking you in business and life. They are the places to put your worries, fears, doubts, and insecurities to be a stronger you under the fortress of God. You will become stronger in your faith to live out who you are becoming and do what you are called to do because you go to the secret place in prayer with Him often.

I remember taking a prayer challenge once that discussed how deeply God knows our hearts. If we truly understood God, we would understand He doesn't just want our happy, all-the-time prayers. He wants the tough stuff. He wants the real stuff. He wants the deep stuff. He wants "the reason He made you" stuff. He wants you to consider that He made you for a purpose, and you can't get there on the smiley, everything-is-great type of prayers. You are supposed to recognize who God is as you enter His presence with prayer and claim He is an awesome God! But, as you are claiming how awesome, mighty, and powerful He is, are you also telling Him your deepest thoughts and needs? Are you placing it all at

His feet, trusting Him with everything you think, feel, and need to believe?

One of the hardest prayers I've ever said was when I was talking to Him about the ones who have hurt me the most. I had to tell Him, in my brokenness, that the ones who'd caused me the most pain were the ones who were supposed to love me the most. I said, "Lord, I know you love them. You know I try so hard to love them, but right now, it feels as if they are my enemy." And then, I wept. I wept to a God who heard me. I wept to a God who knew the whole truth. I wept to the One who I knew truly understood how hard the situation was. I said in a previous chapter that one of the hardest things for me is feeling misunderstood. However, it's also one of the most beautiful things about communication in prayer. I know I'm always understood because He searches my heart and deeply knows and understands me. Because I know and believe this, prayer makes me fall even more madly in love with my Heavenly Father. Time spent with my Father in prayer makes me even more thankful I am His Daughter.

See what kind of love the Father has given to us, that we should be called children of God; and so we are …
1 John 3:1, ESV

Once we have grasped how deeply we are loved, one of the most important things we do is confidently speak that love into the world. It is important to address people in love. This shows the love of the Father, and it is important to do, despite how they may have hurt you or what opposing views they may have. I have hurt others or have been the one hurt when I haven't valued who they are as God's child in the way the conversation is delivered. In an effort to stay real and true, but leave out the hurt, I have made a goal to consciously remind everyone how much I love them and God loves them. I do my best to amplify God's love as I genuinely love people. It took me a few years of grasping at the ungraspable measures of God's love to grow this love so genuinely for others. When I realize how much our Father meets us right where we are, it fuels my desire to highlight His love for others. His love begins to seep in and out of my soul and is a breath of life I carry as an honor to love others so quickly and so deeply. I want to meet them where they are and be authentic in who I am, and prayerfully desire to see them as God sees them.

I want people to feel comfortable with who I am, and that starts by accepting who God made me to be. I want to challenge you to be the best version of yourself. Embrace who you are with God first, and you will know exactly who you are supposed to be, as you serve and love others. Ask Him, "Who did you make me to be?" And then sit in it, soak in the answers and His love, until it's real for you. Ask Him what He's working on in you, the good and bad parts. Ask God to reveal to you the ways He wants to use you, so you can be His best instrument. Allow yourself to be His tool to bless others.

Let the words of my mouth and the meditation of my heart be acceptable in your sight, O Lord, my rock and my redeemer.
Psalm 19:14, ESV

As you solidify who God is to you and know how He wants you to reach others with His love, you begin to shift your focus to praying for others. You can start to pray for words from God and pray for opportunities to have authentic conversations with others. Be ready, as the verse said, in meditation and in your heart to speak on difficult topics, to pour love over convictions, and to break walls in these opportunities by using the words God has specifically laid on your heart. Then, speak it with all the realness and confidence you possess, and in this way, it will actually produce brotherly love when we can laugh, pray, and cry together as one.

*Be happy with those who are happy, and weep with those
who weep.
Romans 12:15, NLT*

This verse is a beautiful reminder of how much the Lord smiles when we are obedient to share our lives with one another. It stirs up a kindred love that comes from this kind of relationship with others. I am going to give you five Bible verses to encourage you to deepen your brotherly love in an authentic way.

• Hebrews 13:1 says, "Let brotherly love continue" (ESV).

These four words are simple, yet they tell us so much about God's expectations of us.

• Another example of this is in Romans 12:10. It says, "Love one another with brotherly affection. Outdo one another in showing honor" (ESV).

Who are you trying to outdo in love for someone in your life right now? I would love to encourage you to play this game with a friend. There was a season when my friend and I did this without saying. I'd show up at her house and randomly bring a meal or start a load of laundry. A few days would go by, and she'd show up somewhere in town where she knew I'd be and bring me coffee and a snack. We'd buy gifts to bless each other's children and did every act of love we could think of without ever saying a word! We didn't ask what we needed, we didn't say what we were going to do, we just served each other with love and kept it spontaneous and a surprise. It carried on at a higher rate than normal. Then, we stopped doing it too often, because we were starting to go broke blessing each other at the level we were trying to "outdo." In the process of serving each other, what we developed in our relationship was a deeper God-serving friendship—one that resembles friends who serve each other deeply, not just in tangible ways, but also as emotional support! We knew we would be there to cover anything we might need from each other. We comfort each other, love each other, and even have the most fun together as Christ-sisters. Take the challenge with someone you want to grow to this level of friendship today.

• John 13:34 says, "A new commandment I give to you, that you love one another: just as I have loved you, you also are to love one another" (ESV).

Through Christ, we have the ultimate example of "love one another." For now, we know the love we must give comes from Christ. But, what this proved to me is that mankind has struggled with loving others for a long time, and it has to be a conscious effort to choose to love.

• 1 John 4:7 says, "Beloved, let us love one another, for love is from God, and whoever loves has been born of God and knows God" (ESV).
I love that this is so simple: the greatest thing we can do is know God and know love.
• Finally, 1 Peter 3:8 says, "Finally, all of you, have unity of mind, sympathy, brotherly love, a tender heart, and a humble mind" (ESV).

This verse needs to be remembered. It's a daily struggle to have unity of mind with others. Even staying humble can take a conscious effort. This is one of those verses to memorize and write in your heart. It beautifully ties all things together with brotherly love.

So, how do we begin applying all of this to our lives? Let me share two examples of when others stepped out in brave authenticity. Two friends lived out the cry for brotherly love by sharing deeply personal stories in full authenticity. One woman shared how racial injustices have personally affected her. She opened up about times she was accused of horrible things she hadn't done and what it was like to be genuinely scared and humiliated. As she shared and asked for prayer, she called for the brotherly love of Christian friends. She asked for prayers to protect against racial injustice in a real way. She asked us to lift in prayer her, her family, and everyone going through these hard times of learning to love and forgive beyond adversity. The call to action was to cover others in prayers of protection, grace, and forgiveness. She addressed the entire situation with a call out and attention to brotherly love. She begged, "Dear brothers and sisters in Christ, please pray with me!" Through her, I learned how to pray for these times. I realized we need to pray for grace and strength in opposition and for both sides to understand the need for restoration and peace within our communities. We must pray for a bridge of togetherness. We must pray for help in coming together to seek God's way in love, peace, and discernment.

Another friend shared her stories of depression and various health attacks that would land her in the ER. She even told me of a time in her life when she'd even written "goodbye" letters to her family. Through her humility, I learned how to pray for her and others struggling with their health problems. I understood how it wears on your mental health to constantly not feel well. I understood how to pray to lift them up and encourage them to keep strong and check in often. I can now see hurt more clearly and pray more openly and deeply because of her story. I now know the struggle a person can feel within themselves because she vulnerably allowed me and others into her story. I learned so much from my dear friend who dared to be bold and share from a place of deep, raw authenticity.

These examples reminded me that the stories of the heart can draw us together in unison. This is the importance of why these stories of the people you know on a personal level make a difference when they are honest and true. Because of the relationship, they make the greatest impact. When you hear these stories, your compassion is moved, your understanding is deepened, and your prayers become more genuine for others.

This is why your stories are needed—your heartaches, your times of rejoicing, and your times of hurting. It's then that we can come together and rely on our great big God who cares for all of us! It's then we are used to shine His glory, redemption, and love on our hurting, broken world. As you serve the world, you are forming relationships. In these relationships, you are creating a cultivated presence of God shining through you. So, shine on, shine bright, and love more deeply and authentically.

My story is still forming, just as yours is, but I now know I need to hit all the points: the hard points, the prayed-harder points, the blessings and the promises I've clung to, the ones I'm still waiting on, and the ones that came to fruition. I've learned how to live in victory with Jesus no matter the current circumstances because these situations will lead to testimonies that change the world. It's not just waiting on the great story of perseverance and success. It's also sharing all of the smaller stories along the way. Don't underestimate the need to be authentic in all circumstances. It doesn't take a special stage to show up authentically, daily to all of those God has around you. Show up daily, ready to humbly be yourself, serving the Lord with the courage to be yourself in full authenticity.

Reflection:

Are you more willing to share your story with confidence? Do you have a better understanding of how to do it in love?

In what ways do you think your story will create more brotherly love if shared with the right audience? What type of audience needs to hear your story?

Has this chapter made you more willing to express emotions? Why might this be important to you?

Do you understand how being fully authentic, not just sharing good, happy stories, builds brotherly love? Are you willing to begin going deeper with your authenticity? In what areas of your life do you think God wants you to share more?

Are you committed to taking the opportunity to pray for others that share their own stories and to tell them how they have helped you grow or brought value to your life? If you're doing this in a small group, share, specifically, how one of the other stories from your group has helped you personally.

In what way will you prepare your mindset to share with an open heart about your own experiences, in a way that helps create unity and understanding?

Does becoming more authentic and vulnerable in love mean there won't be any pushback against the love you have to offer? No, there will be. However, it only takes ten good comments to erase a negative one. Also, please remember, there could be many more that didn't say anything, yet they left with positive feelings when they read it, saw it, or heard it. You best believe and know that it resonated with them to help them grow and produced love, just as you intended it to. Always remember, there could be one person you showed love to that learned how to love another person because of your kindness to them. Eventually, that one leads to more, and the more continues to grow. The more you speak with the desire to leave an impact, the more those affected by the words will live differently. They will share the change that happened in their heart because of the depths of raw authenticity you displayed through love.

When we narrow our focus to impacting just one, we realize the importance of God's deep relationships and how that impact can make a difference because it is personal. It's that moment when you say something, no matter who is around when it might touch one person in the room. God can make a moment and turn a word into a major breakthrough. When we allow God to do the reaching by speaking the truth in their hearts, that's when we see they were affected, stirred, and changed. Then, the hope is that others will put into greater action their new understanding to be the hands and feet of Jesus. Your love could encourage them to reach out and touch others with more understanding, grace, and love. Obediently speaking, as God calls us to, will help others find the truth they may not have been able to hear from someone else. It could restore their faith and renew their compassion to open the door of salvation for someone they love and care about. It is a big, important job to live authentically and to love with real love. Living in authenticity has the powerful effect of changing the broken, hurting world around us—a world that needs more of God's real love.

Backstory

As I see the struggle of finding a space to be authentic in our hurting world, I'd love to share with you how this has developed for me over time.

I remember myself in the fifth grade as a little girl that didn't have very many friends. I was treated with much judgment and learned, through experience, to be quiet and hide in corners. Because I wasn't treated with acceptance, I learned to only share the truth and my feelings with my very close friends—my two close friends to be exact.

I learned speaking the truth upset people and caused them not to like you. I learned standing up for what you believe in was not always the fun thing to do or the most popular vote. I held to that belief throughout high school. I always had the boldness to stand up for what I believed was right, but my raw authentic heart took longer to develop. I made it to college where I had to meet a bunch of new people and join a new church. It forced me to open up to strangers and let new people in. I was lucky to be in an amazing small group in college where I started learning how to pray over the things that troubled us. This is where I began truly sharing the things that were unsettling my heart in an authentic way.

This beautiful heartfelt group of twenty to thirty students was the perfect place to take the struggles I was facing in becoming an adult and step more into my faith. I learned to overcome judgment with God's grace as I was able to share anything that was on my heart. Whether I was sharing from a place of trying to decide between what's right or wrong when emotions clouded the truth or sharing the frustrations of young adulthood, this small group was a great breeding ground to build a heart ready to share truth more boldly and authentically, as we came together in brotherly love to pray over every situation we faced.

When we shift the dynamics of sharing prayer requests from a "facts-only" situation into open, honest needs, we can pray more confidently that we will see a change in the way we had actually prayed for. We will see not just the needs of the prayer requests but also the heart of the one praying. When we are able to be completely honest about the things we are going through with the people God put in our community, that is where authentic love begins to create a Christ-like setting for our small groups. This is an example of the power of community and the building of brotherly love. This is where we get to practice God's love for us. We get to walk through difficult times in life together as we lift each other in prayer. So prayer and more prayer—praying over others and letting them pray for me—is where I began to understand the benefits of raw authenticity.

I'd encourage you, if you have a small group you have been growing and building trust in, encourage your group to start sharing the prayers with the emotional struggles as well. Allow others to enter in deeper prayer with you to build your life right where God already has you. And if doubts creep in, encourage one another. Doubts are real; it is a deep struggle that every believer walks through at different times in their lives. Allowing others to speak truths of how they overcame those feelings in their own lives can also grow your faith. Don't be afraid to ask deep, hard questions. When others share stories of times God provided when they thought He would not, it serves as a reminder of how their faith has grown and fuels everyone else's faith. It is those real struggles that allow others to have a platform to share real stories of God's victories over their life, and we can all see God move in more mighty and powerful ways among His people.

You might be wondering how to grow authenticity beyond a small group setting. For my own path, I began a less scary authenticity approach by sharing my stories using humor. I figured that I could use my mistakes as a funny way to teach a lesson. I love making people laugh, so this was a perfect outlet for sharing the things God was teaching me. I began by creating funny videos about the lessons I was learning through my struggles with motherhood. Soon, I was creating more serious posts about the deep thoughts

I had, and those eventually turned into short devotions. Whatever you use in faith, God will grow.

Even before these videos, I grew my stage presence by sharing raw authenticity with music. Music helped me to always look for opportunities to use what I have to share my story. My biggest advice to you is to begin small. Begin with what you already know and grow as God provides the opportunities. Sometimes a raw authentic post can be as simple as sharing one line of deep thoughts, inviting someone to share coffee or your garden time with or another way to grow can be sharing a stage with someone else who already does this well. Pick someone who would be a great counterpart to your personality. Pray for God to provide the right person to support who you are or the right platform to express your voice as you learn to grow into all God is calling you to be. Recently, I wanted to do an online speech about being "Uniquely Worthy," but I didn't want to talk for hours alone. I met a new friend who was also podcasting and making videos, endeavoring to share more of herself with the world. So, I invited her to join me and share her stories as well. I knew she was the perfect counterpart, because where I am bubbly, hyperactive, and love to laugh at flaws, her soft Southern ways smooth over my rougher upfront edges. Our presence together balanced an audience to reach others on the God-deep personal level we desired. Not only was it beautiful and God-driven as we felt we spoke His words more than ours, but it was also so much fun!

Great things happen when we stretch ourselves to reach the world with the passions and talents God has given us and use them in a candid, open, honest, and authentic way. When we get raw, real, and stretched into Godly places, we can use the platforms He gives us to create something more beautiful than we could ever imagine. When we share from a place of authenticity, we help others experience the fullness of God's love, mercy, and grace over their own lives. Imagine all the possibilities of what God can do when you step into the desire He placed on your heart, whether it is to write a book, make a video, start a business, be a speaker, start a podcast, or even start a small group. Whatever it is you feel God calling you to do, do it with your whole heart, holding nothing back. His glory will be seen in your authenticity.

Jesus replied: Love the Lord your God with all your heart and with all your soul and all your mind.
Matthew 22:37, NIV

Chapter Six

In business and life, you are constantly creating new products, new ways to do things, new marketing, and a new reach as you seek expansions, new clients, or audiences. Creating is a part of growing, maintaining, and keeping the daily tasks of life alive and refreshed. Life needs new ideas and new thoughts to keep your momentum and growth rolling.

What would it look like to create more? What is the "more"? Can I fit *more* into my schedule?

Create with Your Creator

As many times as I have read Proverbs 31, I've always missed something. That is, until someone told me the woman was creating something. "What?" I thought. "Where?"

In verses 13, 22, 24, and of course, verse 31.

> *She selects wool and flax, and works with eager hands.*
> *Proverbs 31:13, NIV*

> *She makes coverings for her bed...*
> *Proverbs 31:22, NIV*

> *She makes linen garments and sells them, and supplies the merchants with sashes.*
> *Proverbs 31:24, NIV*

Honor her for all that her hands have done, and let her
works bring her praise at the city gate.
Proverbs 31:31, NIV

This woman, who is so honored in the Bible as the example of what a godly woman should be, was somehow so amazing, I missed the fact that she was creative, too! As I realized this significance, I reread the chapter with even more excitement as I began to understand what she *created*, she was providing for her home. Wow! One of my favorite topics to teach entrepreneurs is to "get creative," and here it is!

I have been preaching about being a creator of your career for years. My message has been: Take the best of your abilities and talents and create a job tailored to you to serve your community and bless your family. But now, to add to that, I've realized God keeps giving more talents, people, and opportunities to build blessings. As we learn one thing, we use that thing to bless others. Then, He seems to give "more" as we keep going.

Read Proverbs 31 and *all of the things* this woman was doing. And when I say "ALL OF THE THINGS," I mean *all of the things!* It is a lot, so let's dive in more. Let's look at all she has to teach us about growing in the areas of creativity.

Who can find a virtuous and capable wife?
verse 10 [a]

Well, right away, the Bible sounds a little smirky. It seems to say, "Good luck, but here's what you're looking for in a woman!" And friend, might I add, we are capable of many things! I heard this passage was not only an instruction to women, but it was also for men to honor the capabilities of the woman. So friends, know your capabilities and embrace them.

She finds wool and flax and busily spins it.
v. 13

She finds things and makes things. Shout out to all my knitting, crocheting, and sewing friends. But don't get limited in your thinking here as to what you can find and create; this isn't just specific to wool and flax and spinning. So, I'll add a shout-out to my jewelry, soap, lotion makers, and all of those bakers too! But please don't stop your creative thinking there. Shout out to you for what you are finding and creating too.

She is like a merchant's ship, bringing her food from afar.
v. 14

She shops the deals and haggles the prices to make wise choices. She works in gathering supplies. She travels and seeks out everywhere she has to go to get what she needs.

She gets up before dawn to prepare breakfast for her household and plans the day's work for her servant girls.
v. 15

Ladies, we don't have any servant girls, and the kids are hard to convince to do chore work, but that's what I got. Otherwise, we are doing it all: cleaning, cooking, laundry, babies, and more! You, friend, are doing amazing! This woman had *help!* And as you grow, you might even get help too, an assistant or even that housekeeper we all dream about. This Proverbs 31 woman reminds us to grow and bless as we are blessed, to hire out others in their skills, talents, and services as well.

She goes to inspect a field and buys it; with her earnings she plants a vineyard.
v. 16

Are you noticing here she is buying land to grow the business *with her own money?!* She makes investments, and the Lord has favor over her as she expands her business. Man, do I want to be this virtuous woman in all of her ways. Dear Lord, help me move into this position of honor and favor and apply it in all the ways of my life!

She is energetic and strong, a hard worker.
v. 17

Do not grow tired, my friends. This is all going to pay off! Do what God has called you to do and work with enthusiasm.

She makes sure her dealings are profitable; her lamp burns late into the night.
v. 18

She's thinking over business deals late in the night, double-checking that all of her decisions are the best for her family and her business.

Her hands are busy spinning thread, her fingers twisting fiber. She extends a helping hand to the poor and opens her arms to the needy.
She has no fear of winter for her household, for everyone has warm clothes.
She makes her own bedspreads. She dresses in fine linen and purple gowns.
v. 19-22

She's always busy, making something for the family or serving others.

She makes belted linen garments and sashes to sell to the merchants.
v. 24

I think after her home is cared for with all she can make, she makes extra stuff while she's in a creative mode. Then, with the extra, it becomes like a double portion, as she turns and sells it to provide for the house, for growing the business, or for more things to make and reinvest and continue to "create."

But how? Right? How do we really do it all? Well, let's think back to chapter three. We get overwhelmed as He brings "the more," but then, if we work through it with Him, we, in turn, get to produce "the more." Oh my goodness! I have so many new awakenings flooding out of this passage; let's try to keep them straight.

Let's look at some practical examples. Say you are in college, just starting as an adult. For me, that was a time of three jobs, doing homework at 2 a.m., and working on a ranch in exchange for a place to live. But now, as you grow, you take your experiences and learn to apply hard work, ethics, and multiple investments to a new level. When you are looking to build your career or start anything new, it is important to start with step one: What is the opportunity in front of you now? Think about what is serving you, what you can give, and what is reflecting the best of you. Start there and grow. It's all about continuing to grow into all God created you to be. We are growing and learning until the day we leave this earth, so continue to lean into the growth.

I think the woman in Proverbs 31 was also awarded the ability to reach "the more" of her earnings because she was being a good steward of all the blessings God had put into her life. Not only did she make room for the *more,* like adding property and continuing to build her businesses, but she was also faithful with her service and earnings to care for others and her family's needs. She didn't do it for selfish aims, pointed at what she wanted out of life, but instead, she did it to be a *blessing.* Proverbs 31:20 says, "She opens her arms to the poor and extends her hands to the needy," and verses 26-28 continue to speak of the way she pours out blessings to others and is called *blessed.*

The Proverbs 31 woman was doing multiple things: running the house, the marketplace, a vineyard, serving the community, and everything in between. She was serving from a place of gathering all her talents and blessings. For me, I had figured out how to serve in three (actually more like five) of my talents. Lately, I feel like God has said, "Okay, time for 'the more'." Somehow, that shift has felt like a halt; the halt is more like a paused moment of rest to gather all God is teaching me and pull the pieces together. As I look at the woman in Proverbs 31, I don't think she gave anything up. I think her team (servants, but for today's world, I'm going to use the word *team*) grew so she could "create" more and give more of herself in more areas! So, I created a team. Sometimes, that will be a prayer team, and sometimes, a work or project-related team, but they will help me in this shift as we serve each other in this season. The shift of God growing me into *the more* is leaving me in a squat lunge, positioned, ready to run, and excited to do all of the things as I stand on the rock of God. Actually, it's a little more like standing on a surfboard, ready to ride the waves and decipher where to go.

As I move, I learn to do it with God; through trying not to crash and get sucked under the waves, I keep my focus on where He has me. Even this imagery makes me realize the ride is rough, navigating and moving faster than I think. The moments feel like forever, and I remember my one-time, real surfing experience when I was hoping to make it to shore without a major crash in a 100-yard stretch. It felt like forever; it was intense! The journey of swimming out to the waves over and over again was exhausting. The wait for the perfect wave and fighting the ones I wasn't ready for—having to dive through them or under them—was work! And a little scary! Then, I finally had the one I'd been waiting for. It took skill, balance, and a prayer to get to shore without a wipeout. Seriously, intense!

So far, my new career and journey of stepping into this calling as an author, speaker, podcaster, business encourager, founder of ministry makers, and event coordinator for business development conferences has been a lot. I try to figure out if "Faith Influencer" would be a better title to umbrella all I do. Being fully submerged in business ministry has been intense! But, I'm creating something with my Creator. A beautiful collaboration of creation. If we tap into our Creator, who made us in His image and stored up all the talents He wanted us to find, we have an exciting amount of capabilities that allow us to do way more than we can imagine. When we align with God for direction and seek all things without expectation that would put God in a box but with exploration, ready to let God make it into what He has planned, God will direct us through *the more. Woah,* (exhale, deep breath) . . . did you all catch how much was packed in that sentence? Pause. Reflect. And dissect!

So, let's take this in. When we align with God for direction and seek all things without expectation but with exploration, God leads us to all He has in store! . . . Go ahead, explore with God! No expectations! Because expectations put limitations. Trust God has this. Explore with Him, and let Him show you what He wants to show you!

I'm beginning to realize I might be my own roadblock as I'm pivoting directions. I didn't question what God was doing in my last "created" job when I stepped out to make the youth horse program; I just did whatever seemed like the next step. I didn't ask where it led; I just said, "Should I do this? Should I keep going?" Because the provision was there, I kept going!

But that's not the story this time. This time, directions feel a little more lost, and it has way more elements I want to try all at once. The "provision" isn't felt quite as strongly. It's way more like blind faith, trust, and feeling lost. I know God is creating something bigger. I know that. I haven't been here before, and I know this is stretching me beyond the limits of what I think I know how to do. Meaning, I have some more dreams and skills locked down inside me I haven't put to use yet.

Okay, okay, epiphany! Back to chapter three's theme: practice. I need to just practice. I don't have all of the answers, and that's okay. You probably don't feel like you do either, but as we practice the "yes" that is in front of us right now to keep growing and keep creating with God, all the "not yet" areas will eventually come together in God's timing. So as we work to create anything new with God, we obediently put our trust in His faithfulness by just practicing what He has for us to create. As we try out more tools and gifts by putting them to use, it changes our perspective that "not yet" means it's after we are faithful to create "the more."

I'm just a huge believer that we have a lot to offer in this world. We need to dig a little deeper, and just need to try it! We need to reach the more God intended us for.

God's plan to create with you and to use you as a blessing to others will never have an off switch, even beyond the frustrations of any walls and obstacles you might face along the way. You will feel the desire to press further into God and seek His ways to accomplish the dreams He has put in your heart.

A man's heart plans his way, but the Lord directs his steps.
Proverbs 16:9, NKJV

Reflection:

What is something you are creating that you use to serve your home? In what ways are you blessing others with that same blessing?

Where are you serving in your community right now?

Are you still questioning and feeling a little scared and intimidated to grow and create more? Why?

What is holding you back?

Are you more focused on the outcome of what you are supposed to be creating, or are you focused on doing the steps of obedience?

How will you make quiet time to sit at the drawing board with God and begin creating with your creator?

Don't worry, I, too, feel the intimidation mixed with excitement. The only comfort I have is to humbly bow my head, close my eyes, and solely focus on Jesus. It is blind faith when you really don't know what the outcome is going to be but realize He does. You can live surrendered, knowing what He plans is better than you could imagine. I also ask to feel God's presence directing me. Breathe in and out and know He really is guiding this journey. Show up humbly, not "I can't," but humble. Remember through Jesus, all things are possible, and we are humbly grateful that we can do all things through His strength. Say, "I can." Pray through it, for Christ's strength. Show the world the best of you so they might see Jesus working in you and through you. Creating with your Creator should be exciting! Start seeing a world of endless possibilities and create!

Backstory

As I write about this subject, I'm filled with so much hope and so much life still to be had. The dreams I discussed in this chapter are still deeper and developing. One of these dreams is to have land for the events I want to create for others to come to dream their dreams. I can visualize myself buying land and creating the more. For me, the hope to buy the land is a very literal and real desire of my heart. For you, it might mean something different. To understand more where dreams take root, I'd like to share another childhood story with you.

I grew up in a small church in Somerset, California, called Pioneer Bible Church. This church was across the street from the one and only school in Somerset. A strategic place for the Lord to choose, as it served the families and worked well with the school in building a place for the community in this small town. The church was surrounded by a couple-hundred-acre cattle ranch. See, the rancher cut out a portion of his field and donated it to the church. I remember playing Vacation Bible School games in the back parking lot, staring at the cows, and wishing I could own the land. I think part of this childhood dream was not just to be a cattle rancher but to have so much property that a million people could come and experience God's blessings through the ranch land. I've always had this part of me that wanted to give so much more of myself and see amazing things happen for my community off the land that had no restrictions; Everyone was welcome, and there was always room for more. I have dreamed of big fields that are not just filled with cattle, but filled with people and my childhood experiences.

As a kid, our church had amazing community kite flying days, family cow field campouts, massive Easter egg hunting parties, and worship nights at a bonfire, miles and miles away from a real road. A place where the community was blessed by a ranch was a place this child's heart for God thrived. It was a place of love, protection, and exploration! Oh, the massive amount of exploring on acres and acres of ranch land is enough to set a dreamer's heart on fire! I want you to know that's what it felt like to know in the quiet of your thoughts what it was like to walk with your Creator and dream. It's a place of freedom and non-judgment because you are worshiping in the silence of nature. Still to this day, I sit with a heart ready to give myself and my land to a community I desire to serve for God, to hang signs at my front gate saying, "This is God's, and it is for His community." As I continue to pray for how God wants me to live open-handed to serve where I am, I think maybe I'm already doing it. Maybe this small horse ranch, even if I want it to be bigger to serve "the more," is what God wants right now. Even with the small numbers of people and my youth program, maybe it's still growing. Maybe it's all about living out the name of my ranch, 7 Silvers, which refers to God's promises refined in the fire seven times (Psalms 12:6, NLT).

It's the wait and the redefining through God's hands to keep edifying the dream as I reach for all God has in store. It's staying in constant collaboration to develop what He has intended and placed in my path for me to follow. What I do know is that this dream is driven by a seed in my heart; It's a desire to host worship nights, pancake breakfasts, family game days, and holiday events. It's a desire to serve and grow God's family. I'm ready to open my doors for "the more." But I sit with a lack of capabilities because the world around me says, "You can't!" Did you know my own community government regulations are set up so I can't just give freely to my community? Under the restricted laws of how my property is used, they say my seven and a half acres are not enough, and my neighbors would be disturbed by too many people, even if there were only twenty. This past year, I have faced so much adversity as I have tried to serve my community through my ranch. I learned so many rules I didn't know existed. But, because I know who my enemy is, Satan, and because I know where my heart belongs, with God, I know He is behind all the things I've tried to accomplish. So, I will continue to do my part and do what God calls me to do with every effort and obedience. I will continue to build with God and not let the Enemy take me down.

We have talked before about understanding detours and roadblocks as God's protection, and this story is not short of them. I understood as I moved forward slowly to create with my Creator, I needed to intentionally ask each step of the way, "Lord, is this what you would have me do?" There have been a lot of setbacks in creating a ranch to be a blessing for my community that constantly takes me back to the drawing board. Sometimes I wonder if it's for here or for somewhere else, but I also know every step accomplished or learned is paving a road to move faster later. I see the detours as a setup for more growth, and I remember the things that take longer to build have bigger blessings and rewards in the end. The longer the promise is being developed, the more purpose and details God is adding in. This I have seen firsthand. I might still be sitting in childhood dreams, or I might be on the edge of bringing them to fruition. But one thing never changes: I still have the desire to sit at the drawing board and dream up plans with God, my Creator, to plan out His inspired dreams and to desire to accomplish anything He puts into my mind. Even sitting here and respelling this dream in my heart reminds me of all the details He has given me—the tastes, smells, pleasures, and people I am entrusted to love. I am thankful I can give back the blessings God has opened in my heart and through my life.

Keep moving forward, keep creating the desires He puts in your heart, and one day, you will stand back and see that a million sketches and trashed scratch paper have led you to the dream you only once imagined. You will begin to see the glimpse of beauty and the reality of it coming to life. Hold tight, friend. Look up and look at how far you have come. Now, put those hands to work and get back to creating what you have started and see it finish.

Being confident of this, that He who began a good work in you will carry it on to completion until the day of Christ Jesus.
Philippians 1:6, NIV

Chapter Seven

Your calling and the way you lead your life will be an influence to those around you. People will look up to you, watch what you do, and care what you think. How you use your influence to represent Jesus in your business and the community you serve matters.

The word influencer has been misconstrued, and we need to look at what it is intended for as a Christian. Are Christians called to be "influencers"? Does calling yourself "an influencer" get in the way of Jesus? Or, does it inspire you to be an example and keep shining for Him and His glory?

Be the Influence

If you pour yourself out for the hungry and satisfy the desire of the afflicted, then shall your light rise in the darkness and your gloom be as the noonday.
Isaiah 58:10, ESV

As you serve the world and offer the light to others, the light in you grows stronger and brighter. It's a call to serve the world, so you might shine more brightly! See needs, fill needs, know your own needs, and bless others within those needs.

That's a lot of needs, but we need to influence the world. We need to be the light in the darkness; We *need* to shine for Jesus!
So, let's take a deeper look into the word "influence."

The Lord first led me to another word that popped out in the dictionary search, "infectious." I felt I should desire to be infectious. To be infectious means, "likely to spread or influence others in a rapid manner."[2] This word is used most commonly when related to disease, but in a positive way, I want Jesus to be the contagious, infectious thing coming out of me so that others catch His love and cleansing blood. Do you see the correlation to "influence" there in the definition? God's inspiration pops up with directions even in the dictionary, and it amazes me how His influence is really everywhere! Let's soak that definition in. Let's make Jesus infectious so He is "likely to spread or influence others in a rapid manner."

We need to *rapidly* share Jesus. Similar words to influence are "compelling" and "irresistible." Is the Jesus we follow coming out of you as compelling and irresistible? We are to influence the world and show them Jesus is *irresistible.* (Definitions of irresistible: *too attractive and tempting to be resisted. And...too powerful or convincing to be resisted.*[3])

We should work on shining Jesus on the outside, always and irresistibly following Him. It's character development shining out of us. Jesus working on the inside of our hearts overflows to the outside way we love the world and show more of Him.

So, let's look at the definition of *influence:* "the capacity to have an effect on the character, development, or behavior of someone or something, or the effect itself."[4] Well, there you have it, folks. Character shaping is what "influence" is all about.

Our character is supposed to match our Father's heart. Our aim and desire is to live like Jesus more and more every day. If that's our goal—to work on our own character shaping—and we are leading others to God the Father, then, we are influencers. We are trying to influence character development, or at least model it, as the Holy Spirit constantly works in our hearts and as we reflect what a developing character looks like. We follow Christ's lead daily and present ourselves to Him to change our fleshly, worldly ways to match His heavenly ways. We can have the influence to make an impact on others' lives. This impact begins by choosing to live our own lives 100 percent sold out to Jesus.

All Scripture is breathed out by God and profitable for teaching, for reproof, for correction, and for training in righteousness.
2 Timothy 3:16, ESV

Our job here on earth is to share the gospel. We lead people to Christ. I've seen this done a lot of wrong ways, forceful and unloving—"Bible thumping" as some have called it—rather than Jesus loving and leading. I also find people on the completely opposite side, completely afraid to share Jesus at all. I want to encourage you that everything you do is your ministry. The way you run your house, the way you run your business, the way you serve others, everything you do has a place to tell others about Christ and to live as a Christ-like example. Your life is a ministry.

So, let me make being an influence in everything you do even more simple. We are to lead in the way the Lord already made us. You don't need an extra class, additional teaching, or special training. God will use you just how you are. In all of the ways you already shine the light on the world, He is using you, even if it is as simple as a way of enjoying watching a giraffe. Mirroring the image that you are enjoying God's creation—that you share in the love of your Father by admiration of His creation—could lead others to see God, our Creator. Or, maybe it's living out a passion from which you shine out Jesus, and others are able to see Jesus in you. Even the way you effortlessly do your job, showing you were created to serve in your talent, will shine your Creator.

My daughter is a beautiful dancer, but one time, she was moved in the choreography from a center stage position to the side stage position. It broke her heart until I reminded her she was always center stage to Jesus. Then, she danced with her whole heart, and if anyone were to ask her, "Why do you dance so passionately?," she would answer, "Because *Jesus* is watching me." Our testimonies and leadership should shine naturally, as it's just who we are and how we love Him!

And he said to them, "Go into all the world and proclaim the gospel to the whole creation."
Mark 16:15, ESV

Leadership and influence go hand in hand for me. Jesus was a leader, and we can lead people to Jesus. Because Jesus was so amazing, people wanted to follow and learn from Him and get His influence in their lives. Our world can see leaders who are the bossiest be successful leaders. But, being a leader doesn't always mean being the one who is the bossiest. As I've led a youth leadership development program, I've gathered a few key thoughts about the leaders I have seen have an influence on others around them:

Leaders are quiet or loud.
Leaders encourage.
Leaders demonstrate by example.
Leaders are confident in who they are.
Leaders stay focused.

I recognize the leaders who stand out the most and make the biggest difference are the ones who show how it's done by simply *doing* it first. Before they ever have a voice, they have been doing the right thing all along. Others recognized the leadership of confidence by watching them do their job. We can see a leader knows their place in duties and responsibilities. A leader always seems to know the next move, where they are headed, and never seems lost. I think about how frustrated I get when I feel lost and lose my trust in what God is doing in my life and where He is taking me. I realize my own doubts and insecurities are ugly, and I lose the attractiveness of Jesus when I fall short by forgetting who I am. When I forget who I am, I stop leading others. You will be the best leader by being who you are meant to be. You are the best you by using your God-given natural voice and characteristics. You will lead best by the example of keeping God as your leader and letting others know you are following Him in all you do.

As I walk a new path and try to lead in a new way to "be the influence" I desire to be, I need to do something first! Know it before you show it.

What's my something? How do I "show it" in an internet world that I don't know how to use, full of people I don't know? How will I get them to really believe I'm giving them a real side of me? How does God want this side of me to be the example? Oh wait, I'm already overthinking what I encourage others to do, to live life as uncomplicated as a five-year-old, freely unaware of anything but you and God. I need to just be me, be God's, do right by what He has called me to do, and do my best. Over-complicating this gets over-complicated!

If I just keep my focus on God, I know He already is working on me. I trust He knows what the needs are around me as I just try to share genuinely, show all the love and care I can, and be used as the example He desires. With this as my heart's focus, I can trust He will use me.

My youngest daughters are four and six years old. They have a five-year-old friend. We only recently got to know this friend, and right away, she wanted to spend the night. In our evening prayers, my little sweet girls offered to let their friend pray first. She started by telling stories imagining Jesus as a kid, and my littles were talking over her saying, "That's not how you pray." I corrected and said, "Prayer starts with just talking; let's listen." So, she talked some more about the Jesus she was newly trying to get to know and how He had "a stuffed animal and a bunk bed" just like her friends. I laughed in my heart and asked for guidance from Jesus on what this little girl needed to relate to Him, my littles were already correcting again, "No, no, no, Jesus didn't have a bunk bed or stuffed animals! Did He, Mom?"

This opened a door to talk and imagine with my kids what Jesus' childhood might have been like. I asked my girls to pray first, as an example, and to help get the prayers started. Then, I gave the example of starting by listing our thankfulness over our day. Fast forward a couple of months, and these three girls now make up God songs and sing loudly of the love in their hearts. This girl has been confessing Jesus' love over her whole family. "God is alive in heaven and in our hearts!" she tells everyone, and she says it with assurance and authority!

I didn't sit her down and spill it to her all at once. We just live it, sing it, and do what the Bible says, to let the little children come unto Him because they just have this way to gracefully, unapologetically say what is on their hearts. They shine Jesus so brightly. Even if the songs aren't with the best voice, they desire to confess this irresistible love they have found and live in worship all day long by singing hymns like "Blessed Assurance." They burst out with loud voices to sing a song. They just want to praise our Savior all day long. That's what they do. And in turn, it has "influenced" their friend to be sold out for Jesus, even at the age of five!

So, my friends, we are called to lead others to Christ and influence them with the love of Jesus that we carry with us day in and day out, all day long. Influence, my friends, is a leadership role as we "lead others to Christ," by developing the character of Jesus in our own hearts first, then helping lead others and keep loving Him! So, lead on and lead others, my infectious, influential friends! With love and courage to just be you ... fully and wholly loved by God. You are leading others by being *you*.

Reflection:

Do you realize that just by being you, you are changing the world? It is a simple act of loving others with Jesus' love, one action, one person at a time. Who is your "one" God is calling you to focus on sharing His love with more and be that influence? Will you take this challenge to grow your influence one friendship at a time, and one confident, God-given, heart-shown smile at a time?

In what ways do you try to mute "yourself"? What part of you do you tend to hide thinking you have to mimic someone else to be a leader rather than who God made you?

What do you need to ask God for in order to help you relax into the rhythms of His design in you?

It is such a beautiful picture of love to be sold out to the love of Christ. Others will find Him as you live in Him and He in you. Be you, and Jesus will use you! Tell the stories, sing the songs, and live wholeheartedly unashamed of your assurance to know Christ. Free yourself from other influences and trust that God knows the needs. He will show the love that others want. Influence on, my friend. God is using you.

Backstory

Let me tell you about another five-year-old who changed my perspective on influence and leadership.

We moved to a new area, so I had a whole new group of kids for the horseback riding program I run. The students I used to lean on as leaders all changed. Setting a new dynamic of my expectations was going to take a completely new raising of the qualities I expect from leaders in this new group of about twenty-three students. The week had been rough, and I hadn't realized how much my old students, who had worked with me for years, had helped new students know the rules. Rules that say, "When the rules are done, we can just have fun!" Getting to the "fun" of this particular week was more like sitting with the three oldest girls of the group and saying, "This is not how to act. Your 'me, me, me' and 'I'm the best' attitudes are causing fights, and I want you to go last in order to learn your lesson about leading others. I need you to see that a leader puts others and others' needs first."

The whole program is a leadership development program with horses. They are taught from day one that a leader leads from the side. You can't push from behind; you can get hurt and the horse loses focus. You can't walk ahead, because then you aren't engaged in what is going on. You lead eye-to-eye on the side. They were having a really hard time practicing this with their peers and the younger students. The dynamics were three-year-olds to fifth graders. Normally, I focus on the fourth and fifth graders to be student leaders, but these particular fourth and fifth graders came with their own book of struggles for sure.

I'd spent five days speaking on leadership, leadership qualities, and influence, and none of the older kids were complying with what the leadership role stood for. The day before the last day of camp, I would give out awards, and I started watching more intently, all the while praying, "Lord, who am I going to pick for this award?" I was baffled and frustrated by the lack of response and zero turnaround behavior from the fourth and fifth-grade girls. I shouldn't say zero; they were making leaps and bounds in the five days I had them, but they still needed daily and hourly corrections. They had grown because instead of long explaining chats, I had them to the point where I could get them to self-check when I simply asked, "Is that what a leader does?" and then they would make the correction.

But the day of the awards came, and we had our normal routine of readying the horses first. I was still uncertain as to who I would give the award to. There was one older leader I had been leaning toward giving the award to boost her confidence in her efforts, but in the first activity of the day, grooming the horses, she told all the little girls to give her all the brushes so she could go first and "show how it was done." She showed her continued behavior of bossiness and wanting to be the best. She was still stuck in her own ideas of what leadership should look like. Ugh! I quickly pulled her aside and said, "Do you think after five days of grooming horses, nobody else knows how to do it? If I wanted you to lead by example at this moment, what would that maybe have looked like instead?" She looked around at the other three girls in her group who were waiting in line, quietly by a tree that was a safe distance from the horse. She moved quickly and quietly to join the others, but she shoved herself to the front of the line since she still felt like she needed to demand to be the leader.

I'm sure you all have witnessed someone like this, someone who so desperately wants to be a leader they push and fight their way and self-proclaim in an almost screaming manner, "I AM THE LEADER!" This is especially obvious in the childhood years, but the truth is, some people never get that leaders are chosen and observed, and leaders become leaders because of the way others see them, not because of their own demands. Although, I believe one also starts by being a leader of yourself, and even that starts with proving it to yourself. You have to believe in your own heart the value you hold just by being you and doing your thing.

This is a story of just that. As the demanding little girl straightened her face to look a little more proper, I evaluated all the other girls' faces. One had her head down, feeling maybe a little beat up from the girl's pushiness. One was playing with the brushes in her hand, and the last one, the five-year-old, stood quiet but tall, and her eyes were in full focus on me with unwavering attention. I smiled at her and her determination to not let anyone or anything get the best of her day or her moments. I chose her to go first as I thought in my own head, "Let's demonstrate that the first will be last." I continued to watch this little girl the rest of the day, and one thing remained the same: Her intention was to stay focused, no matter what was going on.

I pulled my teen high school team leaders aside and said, "Hey guys, what about that five-year-old over there? What if we made her the leader of the whole camp?" All of them agreed that throughout the week, they had never even spoken to her because she had done so amazingly well. I humbly realized this five-year-old had taught me a lesson: Sometimes the quietest are the best leaders in the room. Her qualities of assuredness, focus, and confidence never wavered, no matter what was going on, even up to the moment of the award ceremony.

All of the kids were sitting on hay bales, and the five-year-old had about five others trying to share hers. Some of the three-year-olds were pushing to sit and falling off, and then they were turning it into a game, but that five-year-old's eyes were laser-focused on me. I got the older group of girls' attention and said, "Girls, look over at that hay bale over there. Do you see the girl in that white flowery button-up? What's she doing?"

They all answered at once, "Nothing. Sitting quietly, staring at you."

"Exactly," I answered, "What's going on around her?"
I don't remember all the answers, but I'll sum it up for you: "Chaos!"

I said, "That's my leader! Hailey, for your unwavering focus, your determination to make the best of every situation, and for being found to always be doing the right thing no matter what, you win the ultimate leadership award."

Of all the leadership awards I have ever given, this one was my favorite because it taught me the most about what it means to lead and influence by example. It is having your eyes laser-focused on your leader. As I remember her eyes on me and how it made me smile every time, I think of how Jesus must respond with the same smile back to us when He sees our focus on *Him*.

Keep your eyes on Jesus. Only then will your focus, your goals, and your influence on others be noticed.

"Because he loves me," says the Lord, "I will rescue him; I will protect him, for he acknowledges my name. He will call on me and I will answer him; I will be with him in trouble, I will deliver him and honor him."
Psalm 91:14-15, NIV

Chapter Eight

In business and life, it is important to love what you do and love how you serve.

In what ways do you love to serve? Behind the scenes or out in front? Alone or with a team? Are you relationship-driven or task-oriented? All of these things are to be considered as you embrace who God made you to be and how He is asking you to serve the world.

Made to Serve

Share you; Serve with your heart.

Each of you should use whatever gift you have received to serve others, as faithful stewards of God's grace in its various forms.
1 Peter 4:10, NIV

When you find your way to serve the world, not only do you realize you are living at your best, but you are giving the best of yourself, especially in the moments when smiling, laughing, and having fun while serving just pop out of you. You have more joy and happiness that lasts all day long. You have energy, and your brain just knows what to do without even thinking. You realize you have found your specific place in these moments. It's affirmation you are using your gifts when other people thank you for what you have done because they know it's not their talent and it's realized all talents of serving each other are needed. We cannot be a one-man show. Serving from your true gifts makes others feel so blessed by you and what you have done. But, even while they are thanking you, you realize it was all just God using you. God was shining through, doing His thing in who He made you to be. Those are the moments that make you feel alive and thriving. For the most part, this is super rewarding. The work doesn't feel like work. It's so second nature; you just click the "on switch" of your brain and go! You learn how to love the people you serve more as you get more in tune with who God has called you to be.

You love those you serve wholeheartedly. You see when they are sad or happy, and you get to rejoice in victories together over how serving them has helped them grow and accomplish goals in their own lives. As you work, you share the stories. They are stories of obstacles you are overcoming or the stories of dreaming up new endeavors. Knowing who you serve makes you want to dream up more adventures, programs, retreats, conferences, and even business opportunities that provide for them as well. In the world of serving others, it is a give-and-take relationship that is built. By serving one, you serve a family, and by them choosing you, you *too* are served. You are truly building a community that cares for each other, builds one another up, and wants to see everyone succeed. When you reach this point, it is not hard to serve anyone, for you truly are serving with your heart.

There are struggles that happen when you serve others and one of the hardest is, sometimes, they leave you. This is another reason why your heart posture needs to work as though you're working for the Lord. It's super important to keep this in mind because sometimes you will only serve that person for a small time. You have to remember you are serving them because God brought them. So, know when they need to move on, it's God's timing no matter how much you poured out and loved on them. As a true servant who enjoys serving, you bring your heart into all you do. So, it is really hard when someone leaves your service, you can take what is "just business" and make it feel super personal really fast. It doesn't feel like just business when they leave your company or ministry and move on somewhere else. When they move on and find a new product or get services somewhere else, it's hard to believe it's not meant to hurt you. Even when you are building a community around you and loving who you serve, there will come a time for that person to move on—I know, it's hard—you have to chuck aside the emotions, swallow the lumps in your throat to not cry and not become prideful trying to understand why you aren't good enough for them as you speak the reminder to yourself, "It's just business."

That phrase "it's just business" can still be hurtful. Instead, try saying, "It's just God's plan." Their leaving becomes easier to understand and let go to surrender to His way. Because sometimes, God wants them somewhere else, and that's okay. Actually, it's more than okay, you want what God wants for that person in opportunity and growth. Therefore, we must let them go and hold them loosely before the Lord in our time of serving them. Another thing to be aware of is those who will take advantage of you. Remember, even in these moments, God has a plan and a purpose to it as well. So, in all aspects of serving others, it is important to keep the motto, "Work as though you are working for the Lord," and this will help protect your heart and allow you to keep serving whoever God brings and for however long they stay.

Whatever you do, work at it with all your heart, as working for the Lord, not for human masters.
Colossians 3:23, NIV

My son started a weed-whacking business at twelve years old. He put to mind that he was working for the Lord and not for man as his clients changed daily. He focused only on the land and the job in front of him. He told me one day that because of where we live in California, and the way it sits on the map, he likes to pretend he's "shaving God's sideburns." We know that the earth is not God's face, but its beauty is designed to reveal Him. What a sweet thought to put to mind and a great example of "work as if you are working for the Lord." You could practically hear his servant heart beating with happy rhythms because he knew what he did was a blessing and that it bettered our world. He even made it more beautiful as he "shaved God's face."

Can you put a spin on your place in this world? Can you see that the serving you are doing is blessing others? The Bible says it is more of a blessing to give than to receive.

In all things I have shown you that by working hard in this way we must help the weak and remember the words of the Lord Jesus, how he himself said, 'It is more blessed to give than to receive.'
Acts 20:35, ESV

I really do enjoy serving others. Maybe it's a love language, or maybe I'm driven because it is an obedience to God's Word that calls us to be "servants of all."

Jesus called them together and said, "You know that those who are regarded as rulers of the Gentiles lord it over them, and their high officials exercise authority over them. Not so with you. Instead, whoever wants to become great among you must be your servant, and whoever wants to be first must be a slave of all. For even the Son of Man did not come to be served, but to serve, and to give his life as a ransom for many."
Mark 10:42-45, NIV

I have loved many through my work. When I don't serve them, and they are gone, I remember the times I had. Because without the service, the relationship disappears. Serving each other connects us in a way that creates a unified community. This type of community is important because when we serve our community, it is as big as serving the world. It helps all the other pieces fit together. When you see the gaps of a need and fill those gaps, the community survives as a whole like an intricate watch: every little gear, aligned just right, does something to make the clock go into action.

In my career, I need to share the stories of why I taught the way I taught, what started the business, and why I valued not only those I served but the way I served! We have to create a place of comfort, fellowship, and service with care. This is not just a fancy slogan to get more customers. This needs to come from a genuine heart that loves what they do and how they serve the world.

Give, and it will be given to you. A good measure, pressed down, shaken together and running over, will be poured into your lap. For with the measure you use, it will be measured to you.
Luke 6:38, NIV

Give lots! Give time, give talents, give gifts, give blessings, give encouragement, give prayer, and give financially. Give when and where you can give. Give what you have, serve where you can, and give where you feel led. We serve others with talents and blessings, which might look different at different times. Prepare in your heart how you will serve and study what God places in your life. Study the people and the talents. Where is there a hole you can fill? Where is the piece of the puzzle you fit best? Even if you think someone else is doing it better, they're not you.

What if you truly believed God has five or more people waiting on your "yes" to serve them through Him? Five people that receive their needs best the way you do it. Through you, He wants to reach them. What if God is waiting on your "yes"? What if your heart's answer was this: "Yes, I will serve as You. Put me where You want me. Lord, I am Your faithful servant; use me as You please."

Each of you should give what you have decided in your heart to give, not reluctantly, or under compulsion, for God loves a cheerful giver.
2 Corinthians 9:7, NIV

It is so important to pray before our actions. I had no idea the entirety of God's plan behind giving in this verse until I studied it. I had been raised to give cheerfully and without hesitation, but nobody told me to be careful of my pulled heartstrings that could mislead me to give in a way I was not called to by God. The line "don't give under compulsion" was a new element, and I realized that only with prayer and wisdom can you practice the difference between not being reluctant and not being led by compulsion. So, friend, I urge you to pray in every moment where your heart feels nudged to give or to serve: "Lord, is this what You would ask of me? Is this the way You would have me serve?" And when you have settled it in your heart before the Lord, do exactly what He has called you to.

Reflection:

When hearing the phrase "whatever gift God has given you," what list of your blessings and gifts comes to mind that God could use to serve others?

Is there somewhere you're begging for God to use you? Is it a particular talent or skill you want to activate more in your life? Is it for someone in particular?

Is there somewhere you don't want to serve? Why do you think you shouldn't serve there? What would be the outcome? Carefully pray if this is your no or God's no.

What steps will you take as you move forward in obedience to serve with your whole heart and work as if you are working for the Lord? Consider now: How will you serve, who will you serve, where will you serve?

When you are serving from where you know you belong, do you recognize the blessing you are to others? List the blessings, as you see them.

Share a time you know you missed out on being the blessing you were supposed to be. How does that motivate you to say "yes" next time God prompts your heart?

"Lord, use me." I just prayed this over a friend who I wanted to serve. I prayed if God was willing, to please choose me, to let me serve her. I realized, when you see a sister-like friend that you think you can't help in earthly ways, you get on your knees and pray, "Lord, I want to serve her. Show me how and use me to bless her life!" If only I felt that wholeheartedly about everywhere God called me! Because right now, considering all my new internet followers, I know I'm still going through the argument, "But how God? That sounds silly. Choose another way." Rather than just saying yes, I'm trying to tiptoe around it, not ready to sink in the muck for the unknown as much as I'd sink for my friend, but here's the kicker: God wants us to sink in, friend or not! Right? It weighs heavily on my unprepared heart all that I might be saying yes to! But if it's God's will to ultimately do it, why should I fear? And then I realize, it's only my earthly fears saying, "I will fail someone and be ill-equipped to do the job." God doesn't call the equipped; He equips those He calls.

Backstory
The Heart and Hurt of Serving

"It's just business" is something my husband has said to me over the years as I struggled with kids leaving the horse program. I poured so much love into every child that came my way that when they left, it was always a sad loss for me.

Some left because the time frame I had for them didn't work, and others left because they wanted more of a competition style that I didn't offer. So, they took their business elsewhere. It was still so sad for me. I see it now as just business, but relationships are what drive me in business, so the loss of even one is devastating. But the Lord is faithful to take us through our weaknesses to allow us to grow and serve more.

Once I understood I love and serve from a deep spot in my heart, I realized that is who I am. That part I couldn't change, so I needed to work from a place of who I was and embrace myself more.

I have embraced my crazy love to the level of "best friends in one minute." I am willing to have a conversation that feels like you are talking to your best friend, whether I have known you for one minute or for a lifetime.

I still love and serve at this deep level of care, but now when they are gone, I remind myself I have given them my *all.* Whether the time I serve them is long or short, I pray they took something valuable from it and that they had a God-blessed time in our presence together.

I leave it up to God to give and take away others in my life. When He has them in my circle of friends or those I serve, I extend love and service to them. But when it is their time to go, I send them away with blessings, even the ones leaving on not-so-nice terms. I send them with the blessing of the Lord to bring someone else into their life to grow them exactly the way He wants them and to fill their needs.

See, when we start embracing ourselves to serve in a way that is true to us, we release others to be true to themselves as well.

Here is a prayer to help in those moments of letting go of the people God has moved on.

Lord, serving people and keeping our focus that we are really just serving You can be so, so hard. Sometimes, there is a family that must go away for a time. Sometimes, this can even be friends, customers, or clients we have grown to love closer than family. Each person that leaves, if we are serving the way You have called, will feel like they have taken a piece of us. Help us serve more freely under You, who You have made us to be, how You would have us serve, and even how long you would have us serve. Lord, when we trust You in Your timing and who You bring and take away, we no longer lose those pieces of ourselves because You fill us and make us whole. Lord, help us recognize when we are serving with wrong motives, wrong intentions, or wrong ways. Stop us when it's people-pleasing and not just pleasing to You. Let us not grow tired of serving others and doing the good work You have laid before us, Lord. Keep us loving and serving under You and through You. In Jesus' name, amen.

Let us not become weary in doing good, for at the proper time we will reap a harvest if we do not give up.
Galatians 1:9, NIV

Chapter Nine

Often, what you feel called to do starts off as a dream and morphs into so much more. It truly turns into a blessing that can have a lasting impact, not only on you and your family, but your community and those who love you.

Do you have a dream? Does it scare you? Does it feel like it isn't happening fast enough? Do you feel like you're carrying false hope? Do you question if you're chasing after the wrong direction?

A Dream is a Blessing

Commit to the LORD whatever you do, and your plans will succeed.
Proverbs 16:3, NLT

I always have lots of ideas I can envision coming to full fruition. At certain times in my life, I would have called them passionate dreams I would do anything to see happen. But as the wait continued, as God held out to not let these dreams rush into play but slowed them to develop, I believe now it was all because my maturity to handle the dream wasn't there yet. I know I had to develop the process of building a dream, and I had to learn to let go of pieces that might not fit along the way. I learned that holding onto something so tightly that you didn't even have yet doesn't leave room for God to do *anything*. As I've opened my grip and held more loosely all of the things God has given me, I now realize none of it was as important as I made it seem. These dreams are not to be used as diehard goals to the point where, while chasing the dream, real life dies on the side. Instead, these dreams are to fill needs, do God's work, find beauty in the world, and be a blessing.

My fight for dreams has taken me through a lot of growing pains. Sometimes, I have become so frustrated with having big dreams, falling on my face, and being left in the grips of nothingness, that I would ask God to take away my heart's desires and keep me from crazy passion. Most of the time, God let me cry it out. I journaled, and then I found something positive about the way I am or who God is to take my focus. Through all the heart cries and search for understanding of what I didn't comprehend, in the quiet of my heart, I continued to ask, "Did you really make me this way?" Somehow, through songs, God reminded me He didn't just make me this way, He *loved* me this way.

I remember one moment, after a late night of tears and frustrations, I was doing the dishes, and Toby Mac's song "Beyond Me" came on. I dropped to the ground. This happy, upbeat song wrenched in me what I didn't know but was starting to understand about dreams. God gave me dreams, but He gave them to me for His glory. Anything I was going to do with the dreams would always be so far beyond me. Until I learn to walk hand-in-hand placing my dreams with God, I will accomplish nothing. And during this particular time in my life, that is exactly what I felt like, as if I was sitting in *nothingness*. This held space of accomplishing nothing was not because of disobedience; it was a time of prepping and heart conditioning. It was a grounding point that was going to turn into a launch pad of all He really had in store for me when I placed it all at His feet.

I had the privilege of going through the book *The Purpose Driven Life* by Rick Warren with one of my best friends. She noticed something I missed. She gathered these thoughts from the book: "Sometimes what we set out to do doesn't actually get accomplished until we are in Heaven!" I said, "SAY WHAT!" I flipped and flipped the pages, and I have spent ten years letting what that means to soak in. Now, I've witnessed lives end, and sometimes what they set out to do didn't get finished. I heard some wise words from a mentor who said, "Sometimes you are creating a legacy to leave behind and to be continued." I see this now as I do some grunt work and build a foundation. As the world continues, God will have others build on a foundation that I started, and the work that is really rewarding is not done until heaven.

Another example of this is Moses as he led the Israelites out of Egypt toward the Promised Land. He did a lot of the grunt work. He successfully led them out of slavery and through the wilderness. Although we hear a lot about the Israelites being stuck in that wilderness, Moses was using that time to teach the people how to be better followers of God, preparing them for the Promised Land. Moses handed the reins of what he started over to Joshua, and it was Joshua who had to complete the assignment. Joshua led the people, gathering territory which would be passed on through generations. Legacies of Godliness are setting stones that last forever, reminding us of all God has done before (Joshua 4:20-24). In a similar way to Joshua and the people of Israel gathering territory, the early church started a movement of gathering people to follow Christ. This work will not end until every person on Earth has heard the Gospel message.

And this gospel of the kingdom will be preached in the whole world as a testimony to all nations, and then the end will come.
Matthew 24:14, NIV

A message and mission you and I still carry today!

In all my prayers for all of you, I always pray with joy because of your partnership in the gospel from the first day until now, being confident of this, that he who began a good work in you

will carry it on to completion until the day of Christ Jesus.
Philippians 1:4-6, NIV

This letter from Paul wasn't just for the early church in Philippi; it is still relevant for us today. It doesn't say we get to finish this work, despite many people reading it that way. It says God will see that all the good work we put in for the Kingdom will be carried out to completion as it continues to carry on after us. He will have each of us complete the steps He has for us. But, there are more steps ahead for future generations of Jesus-followers. I think it's cool how we get to partner with the Apostle Paul, building on ancient foundations, laid down through a rich history of believers who came before us. God's picture is really so much bigger than ours; it's all about what is eternal: His Kingdom.

For our light and momentary troubles are achieving for us an eternal glory that far outweighs them all. So we fix our eyes not on what is seen, but on what is unseen, since what is seen is temporary, but what is unseen is eternal.
2 Corinthians 4:17-18, NIV

Some years ago, I had the privilege of working for a gentleman and training his horses. He is one of the lives I've witnessed that didn't get to see the completion of what they started. He shared with me that he had a dream since he was ten years old, to see black and white Paint horses frolicking in a pasture with babies at their sides.

He grew up a poor boy during the Great Depression. He was around the age of twelve when The Depression struck. His family did not have a lot of means, so he got a job to help them. He pumped gas at a local gas station for ten cents an hour. I believe he kept this job until he was seventeen. He worked with a happy heart at this job, as he was really proud to even have a job. Even in my experience with him later, he was every definition of "serve with a smile and serve with your heart." At seventeen, when he was ready to marry his sweetheart, a man he pumped gas for told him he liked his character. The man asked him if he would like to try a new job and could see a future for him in real estate. Curious, the boy met the man the next day and spent the morning until late evening with him. His curiosity and drive continued, and he learned all he could from this real estate man. "Some good and some bad," he would tell me, as he told me his story throughout my years of working for him.

Long story short, God blessed this young boy's hard work and his willingness to walk through the open doors of opportunity. The boy became a very good real estate agent. At almost fifty years old, he finally purchased the ranch he envisioned in his dreams where he could run these black and white horses. He spent twenty years building a herd that all looked like they belonged together. The original ranch was around 1,000 acres. Back then, it was a $10,000 per month payment he purchased on a handshake with the bank. Many months were tight, and he told me amazing stories where God showed up and paid the bill through sales of land and cattle in the nick of time, every time. This godly man walked on the edge of faith to make his mark on the world, achieving something only with and through God. In turn, he would bless his community through charity, youth support, and scholarships. This man was well-known, loved, influential, and most of all, godly. He never did anything without asking God first.

This man passed away before his final dream became a reality; He lived to be in his nineties, but as he had aged, his family vetoed letting the horses have babies. I let the son know, when he was ready, I'd like a few of the horses. I wanted to see out the gentleman's dream and continue his legacy of letting a baby horse be sold in his name so the money could be gifted to a high school graduate as a scholarship for their dreams. See, sometimes dreams are a platform to launch other dreams and continue a Godly influence in the community. Every single applicant and buyer of the baby horses will know the story of this young boy who walked hand-in-hand with God.

I had a dream to finish out his dream to see these babies and share his story, but it took nine years before the ranch was sold and the son was ready to let the horses go. When it was finally time, I got a one-week notice to come get the horses. I panicked! *I don't have the money for this project. I don't have the perfect fences. I don't have a barn for the babies. I don't have . . . I'm not . . . Maybe I shouldn't . . . Is it a good idea . . . Is it too much . . . Was it just my desire, not God's?* I went into *major* overthinking mode. Then, I remembered some of the lessons in this book, and I stopped. I centered my thoughts and asked God to take this. As I placed my panicked feelings in His hands and tried to better identify the panic, I realized the feeling was the same as finding out, "You're pregnant!" Most women go into a panic, even if they were excited and wanted the baby. There is the presence of those feelings that say, "Am I really ready for this?"

Having a dream can be like having a baby, and when the idea comes to fruition, you no longer feel prepared for all God is handing you. But, much like how the baby grows inside of you, so does a dream. God has impregnated your heart with a dream and a purpose from the very beginning. As you parent and steward His desires for this dream He put in you, you continue to grow with the dream because even when it hits fruition, more growth is to come.

Just like having a baby, you start rolling with it. You make mistakes, learn, grow, and get more prepared. All along, you gather the things you realize you need. Then one day, it's grown, and it's time to pass it on.

I don't know what God has called you to create. I do know it looks totally different and unique to each of us. Even having the dream of owning a horse ranch might have sounded odd in how it would serve God, but the testimony of faith should never be underestimated.

So, my friends, it's time. It's time to step into your calling and go be fully, wholly you—fully and wholly loved by God. Only you do you best! Go. Shine. Leave the legacy. Live out your dream and fulfill your purpose to share Jesus your way!

Reflection:

What are the things you know you have already started that God is using to be part of your legacy?

What is the next small "yes" God is asking of you now that is leading to being an impactful "yes"?

Are you doing something that is beyond your own capabilities, allowing God to write your back stories rather than doing it yourself? What is way beyond your own human strength?

Reflecting on the story of Moses and how he never saw the Promised Land but continued being a faithful servant for others to make it there, how does that make you feel? What would you need in your life to help you be a Moses for others?

We all have a choice to make, we can do what God calls us to or we won't. What will your choice be? Why?

What will it take to follow the bigger picture God put over your life?

Read Proverbs 16:1-9. Put your hand in God's hand, and take just one step at a time. Be still when you are held and move when the door is open. Leave the legacy so when someone looks back they say, "She never did anything without asking God first." Let your legacy be a life song, inspiration, and foundation for everyone around you and after you. If you're still in the battle of the struggle, the doubt, or the questioning, here are some other songs to soak into your hurting, frustrated heart. These songs speak confidently of what we can do because of God.

Sidewalk Prophets: "You Love Me Anyway"
Lauren Daigle: "You Say"

Backstory
Legacy

You really don't know what you don't know. You start your dream, you continue the path, you realize where other dreams intersect, all the while wondering why some never panned out in the first place. Those mares I talked about earlier in the chapter . . . others who took from the herd had babies, but mine didn't. But all of my dreams have the potential for God to turn them into legacies.

This book has been part of a building block to a legacy. Because of this book, I started a ministry to help God's "Yes Girls" keep saying yes. I realized this journey is hard to do alone. Parts of the growing need to be just you and Jesus, but other parts take community and others who understand how hard it is to withstand the journey of the YES.

Your legacy or legacies could incorporate multiple businesses, adventures, family, and 'yesses' that bless others. Keep open hands, keep the lessons of obedience and opportunities for another yes, and keep watching God unfold all that He has for you.

Here are some encouraging verses to sustain you as you continue to grow in your calling and dreams:

Completion in God's Timing will Happen.

"Being confident in this, that he who began a good work in you

will carry it on to completion until the day of Christ Jesus."
Philippians 1:6, NIV

"Many are the plans in a person's heart,
but it is the Lord's purpose that prevails."
Proverbs 19:21, NIV

No matter how long the journey is, God will strengthen and restore you along the way.

"And the God of all grace, who called you to his eternal glory in Christ, after you have suffered a little while, will himself restore you and make you strong, firm and steadfast."
1 Peter 5:10, NIV

He's growing maturity and longevity to all He has called you to, according to His purpose.

After reading forty-eight verses that have to do with legacy in the Bible, I want to share the words of David to his son, Solomon.

When David's time to die drew near, he commanded Solomon his son, saying, "I am about to go the way of all the earth. Be strong, and show yourself a man, and keep the charge of the Lord your God, walking in his ways and keeping his statutes, his commandments, his rules, and his testimonies, as it is written in the Law of Moses, that you may prosper in all that you do and wherever you turn, that the Lord may establish his word that he spoke concerning me, saying, 'If your sons pay close attention to their way, to walk before me in faithfulness with all their heart and with all their soul, you shall not lack a man on the throne of Israel.'"
1 Kings 2:1-4, ESV

The Legacy we want to leave is one that says, "I did it God's way, and I pray I have set an example to my children, and all those around me, to do it God's way."

And return to the Lord your God, you and your children, and obey his voice in all that I command you today, with all your heart and with all your soul, then the Lord your God will restore your fortunes and have mercy on you, and he will gather you again from all the peoples where the Lord your God has scattered you. If your outcasts are in the uttermost parts of heaven, from there the Lord your God will gather you, and from there he will take you. And the Lord your God will bring you into the land that your fathers possessed, that you may possess it. And he will make you more prosperous and numerous than your fathers. And the Lord your God will circumcise your heart and the heart of your offspring, so that you will love the Lord your God with all your heart and with all your soul, that you may live. And the Lord your God will put all these curses on your foes and enemies who persecuted you. And you shall again obey the voice of the Lord and keep all his commandments that I command you today. The Lord your God will make you abundantly prosperous in all the work of your hand, in the fruit of your womb and in the fruit of your cattle and in the fruit of your ground. For the Lord will again take delight in prospering you, as he took delight in your fathers, when you obey the voice of the Lord your God, to keep his commandments and his statutes that are written in this Book of the Law, when you turn to the Lord your God with all your heart and with all your soul.
Deuteronomy 30:2-10, ESV

When we do it in God's way, we are richly blessed. Blessed in His presence, blessed in His love, blessed in His way, blessed by His name.

I want to live a life that makes my kids say, "My mother never did anything without asking God first." I want them to carry the confidence that God is all they need.

As this book comes to a close, I hope you close the pages, close your eyes, and fill the rest of this backstory with who God has called you to be. Fill the space in the world you are called to. Leave the foundation that others after you can stand on what you have begun by fulfilling your walk with Christ and the dreams and desires God placed in your heart.

Where there is no prophetic vision the people cast off restraint,
but blessed is he who keeps the law.
Proverbs 29:18, ESV

To my visionary friends with big, wild, crazy, God-sized dreams: go and be blessed, and bless the others along the way.

Notes

1. Walker, Mel. "What Is God's Favor?" Christianity.com. April 4, 2022. https://www.christianity.com/wiki/god/gods-favor-meaning-and-examples.html.

2. Lexico.com, s.v. "Infectious," accessed January 18, 2022, https://www.lexico.com/en/definition/infectious.

3. Lexico.com, s.v. "Irresistible," accessed January 18, 2022, https://www.lexico.com/en/definition/irresistible.

4. Lexico.com, s.v. "Influence," accessed January 18, 2022, https://www.lexico.com/en/definition/influence.

About the Author

Kendra Dee Carroll desires to see all women live in their passions and purpose. Her heart is to be an example and an encouragement to live out John 10:10 in everything you do.

Kendra Dee Carroll, is a woman of many talents from horseback riding to singing, ranch work, kids' programming, writing devotionals, books, and more. God called her from all of them and to use all of them, to reach back and help women like you conquer all fears and doubts the enemy has put in your way keeping you from living out your calling too! Our God gifts are meant to be enjoyed to the fullest. If you're not feeling like you are living out John 10:10 in all areas of your life, Kendra's messages will inspire you to take your joy back from the devil and activate your purpose and passions to bless you, your family and the community God called you to serve.Hire Kendra as your speaker today and be filled and inspired by her energy, boldness and full out love for Jesus! She wants you to shine Jesus to the fullest, too! So let's restore your joy today!

Kendra is a wife, homeschooling mother of 4, ministry developer, author, speaker, podcaster, and course developer. If she gets any free time she enjoys songwriting and sitting with a good chat over a cup of coffee.

She and her family work together through their horse ministries and rodeo touring life, while running character and leadership development clinics across the country. From California to Tennessee, the Carroll family loves to rodeo, teach and travel to share their passions and talents, and spread the love of Christ around the USA.

Printed in the USA
CPSIA information can be obtained
at www.ICGtesting.com
CBHW030305150524
8593CB00008B/168